THE DECISION MAKING GAME:

An Integrated Operations Management Simulation

Bill R. Darden, Ph.D.
Department of Management & Marketing
Louisiana State University

William H. Lucas, Ph.D., C.P.A.
Department of Accounting
Louisiana State University

New York

APPLETON-CENTURY-CROFTS
Educational Division
MEREDITH CORPORATION

To our wives:

Donna and Elizabeth

6118-1

Library of Congress Card Number: 69-18739

PRINTED IN THE UNITED STATES OF AMERICA

390-25355-3

PREFACE

Management science has provided decision makers with increasingly sophisticated techniques to achieve business objectives. The surprising fact of the present business environment is the small number of decisions which are actually subjected to the rigorous methods of analysis provided by Operations Research.

The Decision Making Game has provided many executives and students the opportunity to participate in a business endeavor and to gain some insight into the problems inherent in applying quantitative methods in business. There is no doubt that many students gain an insight into the interrelations between the functional areas of the firm that is not provided by traditional teaching devices.

Experience in using *The Decision Making Game* shows that students are motivated to apply many of the techniques of Operations Research in arriving at decisions. Many of the features of the OPSIM environment are the results of suggestions made by students and executives; universally, these suggestions have resulted in the creation of a more realistic simulation, requiring more ideation on the part of participants.

The Decision Making Game focuses on Operations Management within the firm and is especially useful in providing insights into the use of linear programming, simulation, inventory models, and present value analysis. Participants have indicated that their ability to recognize business problems has been substantially heightened by using this simulation.

OPSIM *forces* the student to acquire an integrated understanding of the firm's operations. Participants discover the meaning of the systems approach through competing with each other and seeing the effects of decisions on various subsystems throughout the firm. Modern digital computers can now augment classroom lectures with simulated experiences--these experiences providing a bridge between "segregated principle" abstraction and the "integrated realism" of the modern enterprise.

The Decision Making Game is designed to complement and strengthen executive development programs and courses in production management, managerial accounting, cost accounting, budgeting, and systems management. It has proven excellent in M.B.A. courses. The simulation is not meant to replace courses or textbooks, but as a supplement to them. The experience of making decisions and of being forced to forecast, plan and control results in gaining more insight into the management subjects being taught.

Instructors report that OPSIM is easy to administer and requires little or no knowledge of computers and computer languages. Computer center technicians carry out all processing routines after the card decks have been placed in proper sequence.

Some modifications of the game have been developed and shown to be quite useful in teaching game players specific lessons in management. The present version forces the student to concentrate on the internal operations of the firm and allows the instructor to manipulate the industry environment at will. There are ample opportunities for combining game play with learning sessions in role-playing. Chapter IV demonstrates some of the role-playing techniques that have been successfully employed many times at the College of Business Administration of Louisiana State University.

Chapter V provides a philosophy for understanding the role of quantitative methods in relation to executive needs. The level of competence in Operations Research is discussed, and, for those executives wishing to develop themselves in this area, a list of outstanding texts and articles is provided.

Chapter I provides the objectives and philosophy of *The Decision Making Game*. It may be omitted if the instructor is pressed for time.

Chapter II must be carefully studied by the student. The environment quiz is provided for the instructor after the appendices.

A second version of *The Decision Making Game* is provided on demand. Called OPSIM II, this version allows the participants to make price decisions and provides an "interactive" effect between firms. The production environment of OPSIM I provides the opportunity to use Operations Research techniques and is excellent for acclimating students in business administration to the interactive effects of the functional areas of the firm; however, OPSIM II generates a competitive environment useful in graduate business courses including M.B.A. courses.

The authors wish to acknowledge the helpful advice and encouragement of Dr. Fritz A. McCameron, Head of the Department of Accounting at Louisiana State University. Fritz McCameron is one of those far-too-rare individuals who successfully peer twenty years ahead into the future of business education. Acknowledgement is also made to the many executives and students who shared in the excitement and in the development of *The Decision Making Game*.

B.R.D.
W.H.L.
Baton Rouge, Louisiana

CONTENTS

CHAPTER I

INTRODUCTION TO OPSIM

Scope

OPSIM is designed to provide the student with an overall feel for the flows of cash, materials, labor, capital and information through a manufacturing firm. The actual management of these "flows" in competition with fellow students givens the participant a chance to learn through making a variety of decisions in simulated environments. The advantages of making decisions in simulated environments are only now--with the aid of the digital computer--becoming practical for classroom utilization. Some of these benefits are listed below:

1. The student learns through making mistakes--without the concomittant loss in time and risk of money.

2. Business games provide the student with a vehicle upon which to practice his analytical tools.

3. The student in immediately provided with an integrated view of the firm's production processes. This "integrated picture" is a welcome contrast to the piecemeal approach used in teaching production management and cost analysis. It provides a useful complement for most texts in these areas.

4. Early, the participant is taught the role of forecasting in minimizing overall production costs. The importance of the functional areas and the necessity for maximizing the objectives of the total firm are only now being presented through management system approaches to decision making within the firm.

5. Classroom competition stimulates interest in business courses.

In Chapter II, descriptions are presented of the various operational systems which the student firm must manage. It is important to note that the Operations Management Simulation allows the student to plan and control only the production aspects of the industrial firm. The student can not make marketing decisions. The emphasis of the simulation is not served if such decisions are allowed. Thus, potential demand can not be stimulated by promotional, price, product or distribution decisions; however, it will soon become apparent that demand can be affected by production decisions. The scope of the operations of the OPSIM firm is shown in Figure 1-1.

Philosophy and Objectives

OPSIM is designed so that the degree of complexity-simplicity is determined and limited by the knowledge of the player. These determinants are true for the integrated systems, as well as for the individual decision areas. At lower level courses the techniques available to the student to solve the operating problems are rather basic; therefore, the level of complexity is fairly simple. At the advanced cost or production management level the techniques available are more sophisticated; consequently, the complexity of OPSIM increases. At the graduate level, both Master of Business Administration and Master of Science, students are expected to have a working knowledge of the applicable quantitative techniques, including present value, stochastic and linear programming models. Therefore, the play can be conducted at a most complex level.

As a consequence of an intentionally designed environment containing certain characteristics, OPSIM provides many areas where highly technical and sophisticated concepts must be applied and utilized in order to select the optimum courses of action. However, irregularities are introduced into the statistical behavior of several important areas of activity so that the student can not deduce the absolute optimum course of action. Originally, the optimum values for each firm are determined from the same identical history. However, these values are modified by random number generators. Consequently, five firms with identical decisions for the same period may end up with different results. The student must play the game rather than "playing the computer" if he expects to consistently attain acceptable levels of performance.

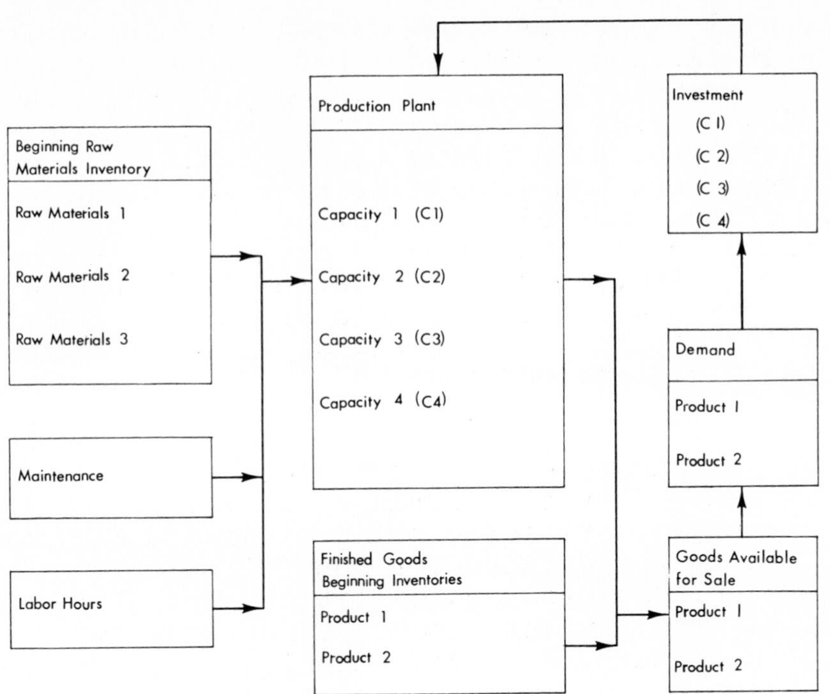

Figure 1-1. The Functional Inputs and Outputs for a Given Period for the OPSIM Firm.

Students will encounter a beneficial learning experience by utilizing the integrated series of schedules and reports which expose them to an organized, logical system of decision making. All of the significant areas of the firm's operations are included in the schedules and reports. Simply by completing the integrated schedules by guesswork the student is exposed to the overall interrelationships of the many different areas of the firm's operations. Not only do the schedules and reports assist him in planning the activities of the firm, they also require him to summarize these plans as pro forma statements and then to analyze the actual results against those plans. In this analysis, the student identifies those specific items which varied from the planned performance.

The schedules and reports do not dictate the values that the student should use. They only arrange the values in logical sequences. For example, the forecasting of demand for each product calls for values to be assigned for the following factors: trend, season, backorders, backorder cancellations and lost sales from previous stockouts. The student, however, must determine these values using whatever knowledge, data and techniques are available to him. Lower level students would be expected to utilize trend and seasonal analyses to assist them in forecasting future sales. Advanced students should supplement these tools with probabilistic distributions of conditional values. All of these analyses are built into the programmed schedules and reports. For the student to determine the optimum product mix under conditions of jointly used factors, he must employ linear programming techniques. Schedule 4 calls for the allocated capacity available. This value can be obtained optimally only by use of linear programming. By using this analysis the student can determine the best allocation of the factors available for the current period.

Throughout OPSIM, both in the environment and in the schedules and reports, an integrated operations management simulation has been intentionally prepared that provides opportunities for the utilization of the most sophisticated quantitative analyses available. Through such planning, the learning experiences available are maximized.

The range and intensity of the learning experience in OPSIM combine to result in a simulation that will challenge all students and, consequently, will elevate their knowledge and understanding along with their proficiency in decision making.

The environment of OPSIM is artificial. This simulation is not a case study of General Motors, International Business Machines nor General Electric--not even Joe and Jean's Donut Shop. It features no particular industry. Again, students must concentrate on decision making based on the given data and not on reliance of typical decisions for the rubber, petroleum or ferrous industries. The environment was designed to provide the student an integrated operations system within which he could apply the problem solving techniques that he has acquired in the classroom. Some areas of the environment are given values which are not realistic. They are planned that way. These values are assigned so that the student will have to be aware of them in his decision-making process. If an instructor does not like the values assigned, he may change them. An explanation is given in Chapter 4 for the instructor on the exact steps necessary to change values.

OPSIM attempts to teach many subjects. The title of the game fully discloses this aspect of OPSIM. "...Integrated Operations Management..." explicitly communicates the intention of covering the operating decisions of the firm. The purpose and the corresponding philosophy of OPSIM are not found simply in the multitude of things. The primary purpose is to place the student of managerial decision making in a simulated real-world environment so that the learning experience of students can be enriched. Through this environmental conditioning, the element of realism--a real situation, a real decision, a real benefit, a real detriment--is drawn upon (1) to capture the imagination and interest of the student, (2) to implement theory into practice, and, (3) to allow the student to live with the consequences of his decisions.

Students graduate from college with the ability to solve particular managerial problems. Many, however, do not have the ability to recognize these very problems in the real world, and, if they do, they do not have the ability to orient themselves to the environment so that they can collect the relevant data to solve these problems. OPSIM is designed to fill this gap between the theoretical ability to solve specific problems and the inability to implement this knowledge to real-world problems.

Other simulations have been written to bridge this gap either in whole or in part. But, nearly all of these games include marketing management. As a consequence of this feature, many of the participants have concentrated on those decisions involving demand, e.g., advertising, pricing, salesmen, etc. Managerial decision making is much more than marketing, even though this area is an important area of management. To force the managerial student to look at the internal operations of the firm, OPSIM intentionally has omitted the ability of the student to influence demand through marketing management.

The <u>philosophy</u> of OPSIM is one of advancement through decision making efficiency--operational efficiency. The student or team who most efficiently makes the internal operating decisions will "win" the game. The student <u>has to analyze the environment and plan the total operations of the firm</u>. Because of the dynamic nature of OPSIM he then has to evaluate the results achieved against his plans. Then he has to start his decision making process all over again for the next period based upon the consequences of his prior decisions.

To reward efficiency in decision making, OPSIM is designed so that the student plays against himself. The activities of any single team affect only that team. There is no interactive consequence of the various teams' decisions. This condition prevents "jester" decisions from corrupting the environment. The teams do compete, however. The competition is directed at the accumulation of profits. The most efficient decisions result in the largest profits. By repeating the play for several periods, the students find that the benefits of sound, long-run decisions offset those results of superficial, short-run decisions.

CHAPTER II

THE OPERATIONS MANAGEMENT ENVIRONMENT

General Industry Environment

The Operations Management firm produces in competition with from one to ten firms (at the discretion of the instructor). Each firm manufactures two products, entitled, respectively, Product One and Product Two. Both of the products are industrial goods and are sold directly to other manufacturing companies. Each firm begins the competition with the same assets, sources of financing, and potential--both market potential and production potential.

The Nature of Demand and Supply. The beginning point for most real-world business activities is vigorous, consistent, and accurate sales forecasting. The same thing can be said for the managers of the simulation firm; some form of forecasting is forced upon the student. If nothing else, the simulation managers must assume that no changes occur from one period to the next.

A few useful facts concerning product demands are available for the use of the firm's management. First, Product One is a seasonal product and has a six period cycle (see Figure 2-1). Second, secular trends are possible for either, or both, Products One and Two. The alert manager should spot these trends and employ them for more accurate predications.

Finally, the potential demands for each product are affected by "irregularities," i.e., there are random deviations around expected product demand, making completely accurate predictions impossible.

Potential demands for each firm are the same for a given period, allowing operations managers to compete on the basis of decision making in their chosen area. However, demand for some firms may be adjusted downward to reflect prior stockout effects. Thus, the student manager should learn more about the relationship between demand and efficient production management.

Model II Demand Environment. A second version of The Decision Making Game is available for use in graduate and MBA courses. OPSIM II has the same environment as OPSIM I; however, participants can

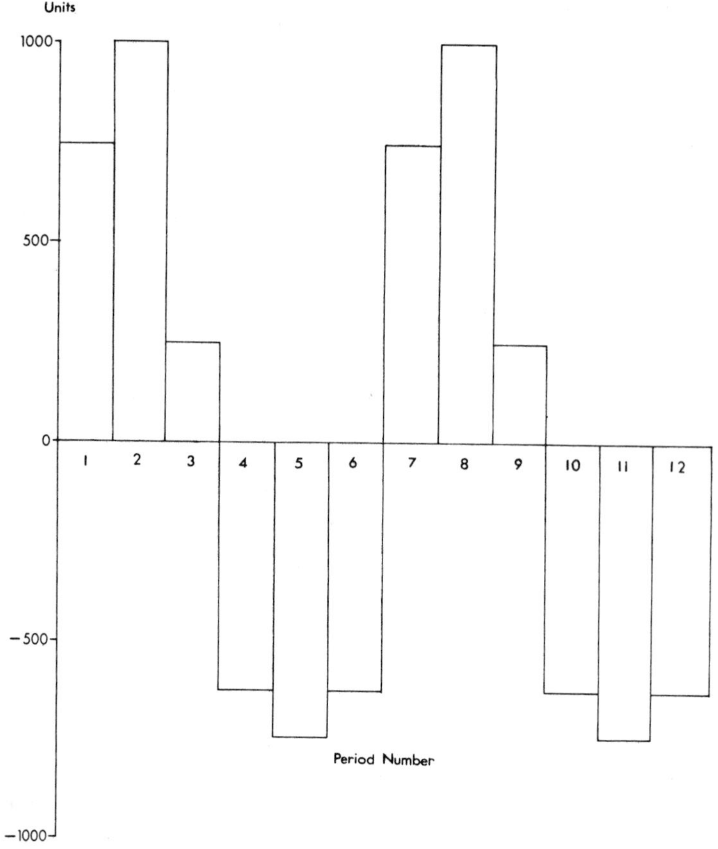

Figure 2-1. Product One Seasonal Effect.

make price decisions in the second version. The Model II game is also interactive to the degree that the price decision of one firm affects the quantities demanded of other firms, and the prices of other firms in turn affect the quantity demanded of one original firm. Chapter IV more fully describes this more advanced game and gives instruction as to how the team is to make its price decisions.

<u>Product available for sale</u>, during a given period, is as follows. The Operations Management firm must satisfy orders for Products One and Two from: (1) the beginning finished goods inventories, and (2) the quantities of goods that the firm manufactures during that particular period. This approach is obviously too simple for the real world; however, the absence of long distribution channels places emphasis upon the decision areas of operations management. For example, to minimize the production costs of supplying goods for a particular period, the firm must consider these factors:

1. The forecasted demand for this period.

2. The beginning inventories for both finished goods.

3. The inventories of raw materials available at the beginning of the period which can be utilized in the production of Products One and Two.

4. The labor that must be scheduled to implement the period production decisions.

5. The production capacity that is available for production purposes.

6. The level of maintenance that is to be generated by level of capacity utilization.

Stockouts and backorders influence the demand in future periods. If more of a given product is demanded than can be supplied during a given period, then a stockout equal to the difference between product demanded and product supplied develops. This "stockout" provides the link between the areas of production management and marketing. From a systems point of view, optimum production management consists of supplying qualities and quantities of products required by management at minimum overall cost.

Management Decision Areas. The Operations Management Simulation requires both current and long-run decisions on the part of the participants. Only through forcing an integration of the necessary period-to-period decision making with long-run profit planning can a proper managerial frame of reference be obtained. In order to make good short-run decisions, management is required to forecast at least three periods into the future. Thus, in each period the participant is required to make both long-run and short-run decisions.

Short-run decisions that the OPSIM firm can make for operations include the following:

1. The amounts of Product One and Product Two to be produced in the forthcoming period.

2. The quantities of the three raw materials that must be ordered. If the decision is made to order a raw material in the current period, this input is not available for use until the following period. Again, a premium is placed upon forecasting.

3. The hours of labor that must be scheduled for production purposes. If 100 hours of labor are scheduled, the firm is charged for this amount regardless of whether or not the labor can be used in production.

4. The number of maintenance workers the individual wishes to employ for the next period.

In addition, the management makes financial decisions including the repayment of debt, and the purchase and sale of short-term securities.

Long-run decisions also must be made. While operational short-run decisions must be made on a regular basis, inevitably management must devote some time to determining future capital requirements. The Operations Management Simulation (OPSIM) allows the student opportunity to invest in all four, or any combination, of the processing centers used in the production of Product One and Product Two. Here, again, the learning experience available is flexible; the student can productively employ investment analysis techniques, ranging in sophistication from graphical analysis to discounted cash flows.

Administrator penalties can be assigned for breaches by the students of game play rules. The maximum penalty that can be given a firm in any one period is $99,999. (See page 86.)

The Internal Environment

In order to play OPSIM intelligently, the student needs some knowledge of the operations system with which he must produce. While OPSIM provides much of this information, the real-world production manager is always seeking more perfect knowledge of the exchange ratios between inputs of capital, raw materials, labor, management, and outputs of products, services, and processed information.

Stockouts. The nature of stockouts in *The Decision Making Game* can easily be demonstrated in the following manner:

1. The amount of the "stockout" is determined as shown below for Product One:

Period 1

Units of Product One Demanded	20,000 units.
Units Available for Sales	15,000 units.
Stockout	5,000 units.

2. A part of the stockout is "backordered" the following period. From 70 to 90 per cent of stockout becomes backorders for the following period with 80 per cent as the expected per cent. For the example above, computations for backorders in period 2 are carried out below.

Period 2

Product One Stockout	5,000 units.
Backorders (.80 x 5,000)	4,000 units.

While demand is increased in the period following the stockout by the size of backorders, it is also decreased by a "stockout effect". This "stockout effect" remains in effect for two periods following the actual stockout. Adjustments to the original potential demand in the second period to compensate for the stockout in period one are made below:

Period 2--Effect of <u>Period</u> <u>One</u> Stockout

Potential Demand for Product One--Period 2	21,000
Plus Backorders (Stockout x .80)	4,000
Less Stockout Effect Period 1 (Stockout x .50)	-2,500
New Demand Period Two	22,500

The stockout in period one also has an effect on the demand in period three as follows:

Period 3--Effect of <u>Period</u> <u>One</u> Stockout

Potential Demand for Product One--Period 3	22,000
Less Stockout Effect Period 2 (Stockout Effect Period 2 x .5)	-1,250
New Demand Period Three	20,750

Plant and Equipment. There are several features about plant and equipment which should be of interest to the OPSIM manager. A discussion follows below on the most important of these.

The capacity of the physical plant of OPSIM is based in four capacity centers. Product One requires processing in centers one, two, three, and four (see Figure 2-2A), while Product Two utilizes only centers one, three and four (see Figure 2-2B). The exchange ratios between capacity "X" hours and product "Y" are shown in Table 2-1. For example, one thousand units of Product One require 70 hours of capacity 1, 25 hours of capacity 2, 25 hours of capacity 3, and 30 hours of capacity 4.

In the initial plant environment, the OPSIM firm has available 2100 hours per period in center one, 500 hours in center two, 1000 hours in center three, and 900 hours in center four. Products One and Two compete simultaneously for the hours in centers one, three, and four. For example, if the production of ten thousand units of Product One is contemplated, it would require 700 hours of center one (C1), 250 hours of center two (C2), 250 hours of center three (C3), and 300 hours in center four (C4). From Table 2-2, the hours available for production after producing the ten thousand units of Product One have dropped considerably (for example: the hours in center one have dropped from 2100 hours to 1400 hours). However, 37.5 thousand units of Product Two can still be produced (1400/30 = 46.7, 7500/20 = 37.5, 600/15 = 40).

Table 2-1

The company is producing Products One and Two utilizing four different types of equipment. Capacity 1 is determined by a general lathe. Capacity 2 corresponds to a special lathe which is only used on Product One. Capacity 3 is determined by a milling machine, and a drill press determines capacity 4. The matrix below illustrates the relationships between the equipment and the products.

Y

	One Thousand Units--Product One	One Thousand Units--Product Two	Total
Capacity 1	70 hours	30 hours	2100 hours
Capacity 2	25	0	500
Capacity 3	25	20	1000
Capacity 4	30	15	900

Table 2-2

Hours Available for Production
After Producing Product One

	Center One	Center Two	Center Three	Center Four
Total Hours Available	2100	500	1000	900
Hours Needed for Ten Thousand Units of Product One	700	250	250	300
Hours Available for Additional Production	1400	250	750	600

If management wishes to produce 37.5 thousand units of Product Two (after Producing ten thousand units of Product One), the hours needed, and the hours remaining after production, are shown in Table 2-3. All the hours in center three have now been utilized and further production is impossible, since the production of a unit of either Product One or Product Two requires center three.

The utilization of the plant and equipment capacities are subject to some programmed constraints. Since the products of OPSIM are components used for production by other industrial firms, orders are received and filled in the current period out of period beginning inventory and current production. Figures 2-2A and 2-2B illustrate this "availability" from a schematic view.

Moreover, once the production decisions for a period have been made, the actual production process has the following priorities:

1. All inputs (labor, raw materials, capacities, etc.) are first used to produce Product One.

2. After Producing Product One, the remaining inputs are used to produce Product Two.

3. If the company wishes to produce more of Products One and Two than it has inputs to produce, then the simulation produces only as much as the maximum output allowed by the constraint resource needed in production. Thus, the OPSIM management must forecast into the future to ascertain inventory requirements to offset limited production ability.

Table 2-3

Hours Available After Producing Product Two

	Center One	Center Two	Center Three	Center Four
Hours Available After Producing Product One	1400	250	750	600
Hours to Produce 37.5 Units of Product Two	1125	0	750	562
Hours of Unused Capacity	275	250	0	38

The OPSIM firm has found that due to the special characteristics of its facilities, regardless of the circumstances, it is always more profitable to follow the above production priorities. Specifically, the machine setup cost for Product One reduces the setup cost for Product Two so significantly that Product One is always run first. The consideration to OPSIM management is the fact that resources are first used in implementing the Product One production decision and only those inputs remaining after this production can be used to produce Product Two.

Investment in equipment by the OPSIM manager for any of the plant processing centers is allowed. For example, management could decide to invest in center three since, in the example given in the

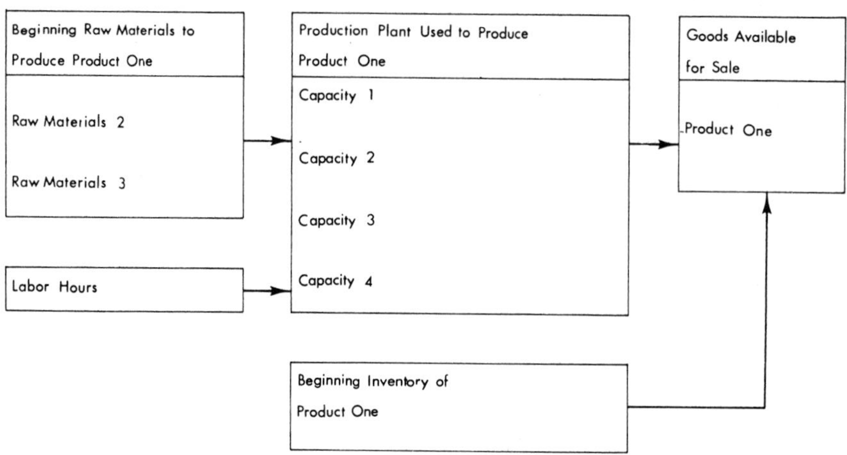

Figure 2-2A. Material and Capacity Centers Needed to Produce Product One.

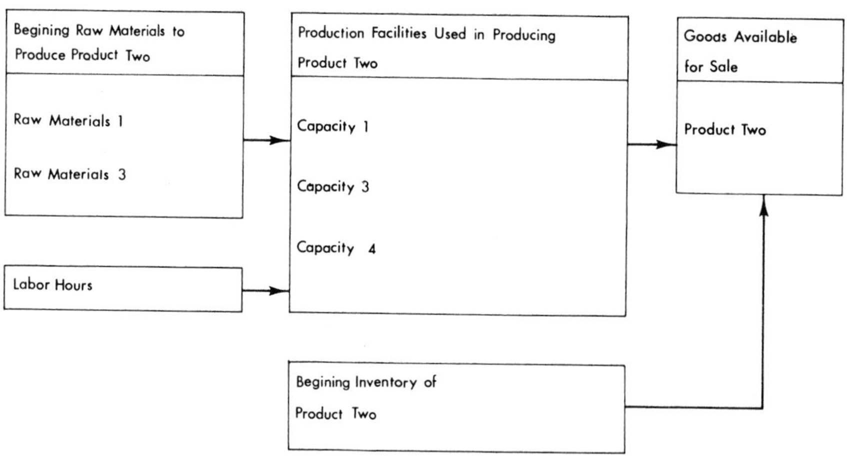

Figure 2-2B. Material and Capacity Centers Needed to Produce Product Two.

last section, the further production of either Product One or Product Two is restricted by lack of capacity in this center. However, the minimum investment in any center--if any investment is to be made--is equal to the initial center capacity. In center three, the original capacity is 1000 hours per period; therefore, the minimum hours that can be purchased is 1000 additional hours. The student should think of each center as initially representing a processing machine and additional investment requires buying similar machines. Thus, the capacity that is possible to be purchased in any given center is a full multiple of original period capacity. For example, in any period management can invest in 1000, 2000, or 3000 hours of center three. The same type of analysis is true for centers one, two, and four.

The investment price and depreciation charges are of special interest to the OPSIM manager. The decision to invest involves outlays of cash for machines and the projected additional net cash flows made possible by the sales of additional products. In Table 2-4 is shown the price per investment unit for each processing center. When entering the decision, management can: (1) choose not to invest (indicated by a "0" for each center), (2) decide to invest in one unit of one or all machine centers (indicated in the decision format by a "1"), or (3) invest in multiple units of each center (shown in format by whole numbers higher than "1").

Investment is automatically financed by debt, which is initially carried at 2% interest per period (note: this is 24% per annum). Indirectly, investment can be financed by retained earnings through the following procedure:

1. Invest in the desired centers, automatically incurring debt.

2. Simultaneously make a "payments" decision and an investment decision; therefore, debt is reduced at the same time it is incurred and no interest is charged.

Since the life of a unit of investment is one hundred playing periods, under most circumstances no machine is ever fully depreciated during even the longest number of playing periods. Depreciation is computed using a straight line method; therefore, depreciation per machine, per period is one one-hundredth of the initial price.

Table 2-4

Price and Hours That Result From One Investment Unit In Centers One, Two, Three, and Four.

	Hours Per Unit	Unit Purchase Price	Number of Machines
Center One	2100	$150,000	1
Center Two	500	$100,000	1
Center Three	1000	$150,000	1
Center Four	900	$100,000	1

Raw Materials System. The acquisition of raw materials is perhaps the most important aspect of the raw materials system. All raw materials used in the production of Product One and Product Two must be in beginning inventories for the period during which production is contemplated. All order decisions, made for that period, are received at the end of the period and are available for production in subsequent periods. The example below in Table 2-5 illustrates the changes in raw material inventories from one period to the next.

The inventory valuation of raw materials is determined using a modified first-in first-out cost flow method. Since the OPSIM firm only uses materials from beginning inventories, management has no problem in costing raw materials used in production. However, the price of raw materials received at the end of the period may be different from materials that are used during the operating span. The OPSIM firm solves this problem by taking a weighted average of unused materials and orders received to arrive at a new per unit ending inventory valuation. Since ending inventory becomes next period's beginning inventory, product materials cost in the following period is computed using this weighted price.

Raw material prices vary, and management may find speculating to be profitable. The student manager should recognize, however, that large average inventories have to be stored, insured, etc., resulting in carrying costs which may offset any speculative savings in periods of increasing prices.

Table 2-5

Unit Changes in Raw Materials Inventories

	Raw Material 1	Raw Material 2	Raw Material 3
Period 1 Beginning Inventory	300,000	300,000	227,500
Raw Materials Used in Period 1	-275,000	-250,000	-227,500
Unused Materials in Period 1	25,000	50,000	0
Plus Orders in Period 1	250,000	250,000	200,000
Ending Inventory Period 1: Inventory Available for Production Period 2	275,000	300,000	200,000

Order and carrying costs of materials play an important role in raw material decisions. Each raw material has both an order cost and a carrying cost. The OPSIM firm's raw material order cost varies directly with the number of orders for a given year, and its carrying cost varies directly with the size of average inventory. These relationships allow management to analyze the costs involved in ordering and maintaining inventories and to gain experience in developing and utilizing standard economic order quantity models. From simulation experience, student managers learn both the strengths and inadequacies of standard inventory models. Further, management learns to adopt inventory models to its own special environments. Table 2-6 shows the carrying costs and order costs for each raw material used in OPSIM.

Table 2-6

Carrying and Order Costs for Raw Materials

	Raw Material 1	Raw Material 2	Raw Material 3
Period Carrying Cost Per Unit of Average Inventory	$ 00.10	$ 00.11	$ 00.09
Cost Per Order of Raw Material	1500.00	2000.00	2000.00

Materials Requirement for production for both products are shown in Table 2-7. One unit of Product One requires exactly 40 units of material 2 and approximately 10 units of material 3.

Table 2-7

Materials and Labor Requirements for Products One and Two

	Product One	Product Two
Material 1		25 units
Material 2	40 units	
Material 3	10 units	15 units
Labor	.28 hours	.20 hours

Also, a single unit of Product Two requires _exactly_ 25 units of material 1 and _approximately_ 15 units of material 3. Management in the OPSIM environment finds that materials 1 and 2 are highly reliable--that is the quality of these materials is so high that exact prognostications about their input-output exchange ratios can be made; however, material 3 is not so reliable. The number of units of this input required to produce one unit of output is a random variable, sometimes requiring as little as 90% and sometimes as much as 110% of the _expected_ ratios listed in Table 2-7. Productions requirements for material 3, then, is sometimes lower than expected, but sometimes higher than expected. Thus, management is faced with input variance, and in the case where material 3 is the constraint resource (in short supply in relation to production requirements), it is also faced with output variance (more or less output than expected).

Labor Requirements. The number of labor hours needed for the desired level of production must be scheduled at the beginning of each period. Once labor has been scheduled, each scheduled hour is charged to the firm, regardless of whether or not all these hours are used. Table 2-7 indicates that .28 and .20 hours, respectively, are needed for the production of a single unit of Products One and Two. "Benefits" per labor hour can also be exacted by the game administrator, facilitating "role playing" in collective bargaining. Initially each labor hour costs $4.50.

The Maintenance System. The OPSIM production centers require maintenance. In the OPSIM environment, management can hire as many maintenance workers as it wishes for each period. The cost of maintenance workers is a "period" cost, and worker cost is the only cost involved in any preventive maintenance activities. Maintenance cost, then, is composed of three elements: first, the cost of maintenance workers engaged in preventive and breakdown activities; second, the actual cost of breakdown maintenance; and third, the capacity hours lost due to breakdown. Figure 2-3 shows the relationship between the number of workers and breakdown maintenance cost. Hiring more maintenance workers reduces breakdown maintenance cost up to a point; however, the total maintenance worker cost is increasing at the same time. Management can minimize total maintenance cost by hiring workers up to the point where worker cost plus breakdown maintenance cost is a minimum.

In the OPSIM production environment, the level of the maintenance cost function varies directly with the amount of capacity hours used during a given period (see the dotted curve in Figure 2-3). The OPSIM manager learns to make decisions on the basis of hypotheses, to evaluate feedback in the forms of operating statements

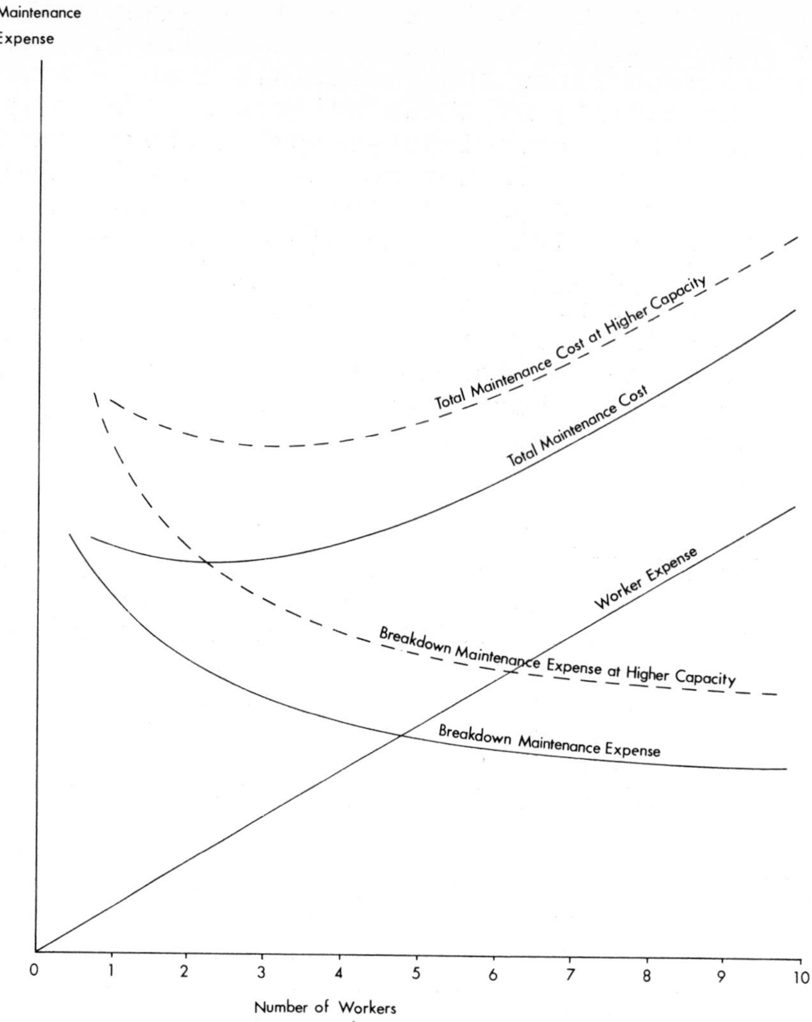

Figure 2-3. Maintenance Expense Analysis.

and accounting data, and to revise these operating hypotheses in the light of additional information gained from the analysis of this historical information. Each worker costs $500 per period.

In addition to maintenance expenses, the OPSIM firm is subject to random breakdowns. However, the actual hours lost due to a breakdown are inversely related to the number of maintenance workers hired for that period. Regardless of the hours lost in a breakdown for a period, in the following period the machine that was broken is assumed to be in full operation. (See page 91.)

Finished Goods System. Setup costs are incurred in each period the OPSIM manager decides to produce. The decision to produce either Product One or Product Two, or both products, results in a setup cost for a given period (if both products are produced, separate setup costs are incurred for each). The OPSIM manager is limited in the time span for which a production run can be set up. He can only set up to produce during a given period, and the size of the production run is limited by the available capacity for that period. Setup costs for a period run are composed of paperwork, machine settings, and gearing-up costs in general. The respective setup cost for the products are shown in Table 2-8.

Carrying cost for each product is based on cost per unit of average inventory. Thus, as average inventory for a product becomes larger, the total carrying cost for that good also increases. The knowledge of "average" inventory, then, becomes quite important to the OPSIM manager in minimizing cost. Average inventory is one-half of the sum of the product beginning inventory and its ending inventory. An example of how the company in the OPSIM industry computes average inventory and carrying cost for Product Two is given below.

Product Two

I.	Beginning Inventory (units)................	20,000 units
II.	Ending Inventory (units)..................	+22,000 units
III.	Sum of Beginning and Ending Inventories (I + II)...................	42,000 units
IV.	Average Inventory (III divided by 2)................................	21,000 units
V.	Cost Per Period Per Unit Average Inventory......................	$ 0.15/unit/period
VI.	Carrying Cost for the Period (IV x V)...........................	$ 3,150/period

The initial carrying costs per unit of average inventory and the setup costs for Products One and Two are shown in Table 2-8. Through careful demand forecasting, management uses such data to help make more optimal production scheduling decisions.

Table 2-8

Setup Cost and Initial Carrying Cost Per Unit of Average Inventory

	Product One	Product Two
Unit Carrying Cost	$ 00.20	$ 00.15
Setup Cost	5000.00	6000.00

The <u>inventory valuation</u> for all OPSIM firms is determined by using a <u>modified FIFO method</u> of inventory valuation. During any period, orders for either product are first supplied out of beginning inventory. If product demand is greater than beginning inventory, the difference between orders and initial inventory is supplied out of current production.

The cost of orders corresponds to the source of supply; therefore, the cost of orders supplied out of beginning inventory is valued at unit beginning inventory values. Moreover, residual orders which are supplied out of current production have current production unit costs.

The computation of the unit cost of ending inventory, however, involves a weighted average of the beginning inventory which remains, and current production. The example of Product One below should clarify this method of costing.

Product One

I. Beginning Inventory (Unit Cost- $55/Unit)............................ 30,000 units

II.	Orders of Product One	20,000 units
III.	Unused Beginning Inventory ($55/Unit)	10,000 units
IV.	Current Production ($60/Unit)	20,000 units
V.	Ending Inventory	30,000 units

The unit cost of ending inventory (which becomes the unit cost of beginning inventory for the following period) is computed in the following fashion:

C_C = Unit Cost of Current Production
C_E = Unit Cost of Ending Inventory
C_B = Unit Cost of Beginning Inventory
Q_B = Unused Units of Beginning Inventory
Q_C = Unused Units of Current Production
Q_E = Units in Ending Inventory

$$C_E = \frac{Q_B \cdot C_B + Q_C \cdot C_C}{Q_B + Q_C} = \frac{10{,}000 \text{ x } \$55 + 20{,}000 \text{ x } \$60}{10{,}000 + 20{,}000}$$

$C_E = \$58.33$
$Q_E = Q_B + Q_C = 10{,}000 \text{ units} + 20{,}000 \text{ units}$
$Q_E = 30{,}000 \text{ units}$

The OPSIM firm has no in-process inventories. Management completes the production of a run in the period in which it is begun and at the period's end only finished goods inventories (as well as raw materials inventories) exist.

OPSIM Financial System. The sources of capital for companies operating in the OPSIM industry are initially limited to equity. Since all accounts are paid promptly, there are no accounts-payable at the end of each period. If not enough cash is available to pay all the firm's accounts, the company has access to funds through borrowing on an open line of credit at the bank. Thus, debt is automatically incurred by the firm in two circumstances:

1. The firm's prompt payment policy requires that, if necessary, it must borrow to pay all accounts. Therefore, when the cash outflows are greater than the cash available, the OPSIM firm goes into a debt position for the amount of the deficit.

2. When the company invests in machines for the various pro-

cessing centers, as already indicated, these investment decisions are financed by debt. However, if a firm has generated sufficient cash reserves through retained earnings, effective investment of retained earnings can be accomplished by simultaneously making two decisions: first, management can make the decision to invest "x" amount of dollars; and second, the decision makers can make payments on debt for "x" amount of dollars. The net effect of the above strategy is no increase in debt, an increase in productive assets, and a decrease in cash assets.

The period debt position during a given period, which is the amount upon which interest is charged, is equal to last period's debt minus current debt payments plus current borrowing to pay outstanding accounts plus current investment in machines. The OPSIM firm must pay interest on current debt investment funds; however, since the investment decision is made in the current period and installation must take place, the machines can not be used until the following period. Also, the firm does not claim depreciation on current investment until next period.

The rate of interest and method of debt payment affect the operations of the OPSIM firm. The source of debt funds is unlimited, but the cost of debt is initially equal to a rate of interest of 2% per period (24% per annum). The OPSIM firm can borrow for any length of time and termination of debt (and the interest charged for debt) occurs only with the decision to pay off debt. At any time, part, or all, of the debt outstanding can be paid off if the company has generated sufficient cash reserves.

Short-term securities may be purchased by the OPSIM firm when it has excess cash reserves on hand, earning 1.5% per period.

The cash flows from operations are determined as follows. The cash position of any firm at the end of a current decision period is beginning cash less current expenses plus approximately 75% of current sales, plus the beginning balance of accounts receivables (which are all collected in the current period). The per cent of current sales which is realized in cash during a period randomly varies from 70 per cent to 80 per cent (with 75 per cent of sales being the expected cash receipts). The remaining sales become accounts receivable for the current period and are to be collected in the following period.

Reports Provided to the OPSIM Manager

Production management needs special reports to facilitate both the planning and the controlling of all operations. The OPSIM manager has several reports provided to each firm at the end of every period. These reports are the only feedback the student manager has concerning the effectiveness and efficiency of prior decisions. In order to compete successfully, management must learn to interpret and extrapolate on the basis of information contained in the following reports:

1. A managerial operating statement based on direct costing procedures.

2. A traditional absorption operating statement.

3. A running balance sheet, to show the firm's asset position at the end of each period.

4. Other marketing and accounting information needed for forecasting, planning, and controlling purposes.

5. An industry report showing competitive positions.

A Prototype Production Decision

An example illustrates the inputs that must be considered in any production decision. Management desires to produce one thousand units of Product One and one thousand units of Product Two. The inputs needed to produce this scheduled production are shown in Table 2-9. Thus, 100 hours of capacity 1, 25 hours of capacity 2, 45 hours of capacity 3, 45 hours of capacity 4, 25,000 units of raw materials 1, 40,000 units of raw materials 2, 25,000 units of raw materials 3 and 480 hours of labor are all required to produce the desired quantities of Products One and Two in the current period. The capacity input-output exchange ratios used in Table 2-9 are drawn from Table 2-1, which shows the number of hours of a given capacity needed to produce one thousand units of either Product One or Product Two. Table 2-7 provides the needed raw material and labor product exchange ratios.

Row one in Table 2-10 shows the various quantities of inputs that are <u>available</u> for production purposes, while row two reproduces the <u>inputs</u> required to implement production plans. If, in any column, the quantity of input available is less than the quantity of input required, then plans can not be fully implemented. Planned production is reduced according to the priorities established in a prior section of this chapter. In Table 2-10 there are no constraint inputs; therefore, planned production can take place.

However, a great deal of capacity is unused and raw materials inventories are unusually large. If current production plans are the best under the circumstances, the prior investment and materials ordering decisions may have been poor. Management should always balance out the risk of stockout versus the investment and inventory carrying costs.

Table 2-9

Required Inputs	I *C-1 in hrs	II C-2 in hrs	III C-3 in hrs.	IV C-4	V Raw **Mat. 1 units	VI Raw Mat. 2 units	VII Raw Mat. 3 units	VIII Labor hrs
Pro-duct 1	1x70	1x25	1x25	1x30		40x 100	10x 100	.28x 1000
	70	25	25	30	-0-	40000	10000	280
Pro-duct 2	1x30	1x0	1x20	1x15	25x 1000		15x 1000	.20x 1000
	30	-0-	20	15	25000	-0-	15000	200
Total	100	25	45	45	25000	40,000	25000	480

*C=Capacity
**Mat.=Material

Table 2-10

	I	II	III	IV	V	VI	VII	VIII
	*C-1 in hrs	C-2 in hrs	C-3 in hrs	C-4 in hrs	Raw **Mat. 1 units	Raw Mat. 2 units	Raw Mat. 3 units	Labor in hrs
Inputs Available	2100	500	1000	900	380,000	300,000	300,000	480
Inputs Required	100	25	45	45	25,000	40,000	25,000	480
Unused Inputs	2000	475	955	855	275,000	260,000	275,000	-0-

*C = Capacity
**Mat. = Material

CHAPTER III

OPSIM DECISION MAKING

The Decision-Making Process: An Overview.

The OPSIM manager faces the challenge of running the entire operations of the firm. Individually, or as a member of the management team, he is charged with the responsibility of optimally managing the activities of the firm.

For the firm, this includes decisions for each of the many different activities broadly classified as selling, producing, and financing. If any one area is overlooked or is haphazardly planned, the consequence is felt throughout the firm. After decisions are determined for specific activities, the manager must integrate them into an optimum master plan for the period. Any decision not consistent or compatible with the master plan must be modified. The decisions for the current period must be further reviewed to assure that they attempt to maximize the long-run objectives of the firm.

For the OPSIM company, the maximization of profits is the desired objective. The means available to achieve this goal are efficiencies in decision making. The ability of the manager to select the optimum courses of action is reflected in the profits his firm makes and consequently, he is evaluated on this criterion.

Once the operating decisions have been made, the manager schedules the acquisition and utilization of the production factors which constitute the operating budgets for the respective areas. From these schedules the cash budget for the period is prepared.

If the available cash is short of the scheduled use of cash, the manager must either reduce his planned level of activities or borrow funds. If an excess of funds exists, management should evaluate the alternative uses of it.

The total planned activities are then summarized in *pro forma* financial statements. Here, the budgeted contribution margin and contribution for the period, as well as the anticipated financial position at the end of the period are spelled out in detail. At the end of the period the manager should compare the budgeted to the actual results and analyze the differences; thereby, he identifies the weaknesses in his decision-making process. To increase the efficiency of his decision-making ability, the manager should evaluate his techniques in the areas where deviations occur. Perhaps the techniques being used are sound and are the best available, and if this is the case, the manager should try to define the limits of the behavior of the activity. Through such analysis the manager gains knowledge of the reliability of his decisions. Consequently, he must build in safety stocks to allow for "known" erroneous decisions.

On the other hand, the manager may be using poor techniques to determine his course of action. The student, in this case, has his attention directed to deficiencies in his decision-making ability and would, therefore, be expected to review the specific area in the textbook.

The specific input decisions which the OPSIM manager must make and the respective units of account are as follows:

Item	Decision Areas	Unit of Account
1.	Production of Product One	Products
2.	Production of Product Two	Products
3.	Acquisition of Raw Material 1	Pounds
4.	Acquisition of Raw Material 2	Pounds
5.	Acquisition of Raw Material 3	Pounds
6.	Acquisition of Direct Labor Hours	Hours
7.	Acquisition of Maintenance Labor Workers	Workers
8.	Investment in Capacity One	Machines
9.	Investment in Capacity Two	Machines
10.	Investment in Capacity Three	Machines
11.	Investment in Capacity Four	Machines
12.	Repayment of Debt	Dollars
13.	Investment in Short-Term Securities	Dollars
14.	Sale of Short-Term Securities	Dollars

To assist the OPSIM manager in developing his decision-making ability, a series of integrated schedules and reports are provided for him to complete. These schedules have been prepared so that the student comprehensively determines the courses of action that his firm undertakes. At the same time, the schedules are arranged in a logical order for decision making. The utilization of some of these forms is explained and illustrated in the next section of this chapter. At the end of this manual a supply of these forms is provided for the student to use each period.

When the decisions have all been made, their consequences are determined by the use of the digital computer. Each period these results are prepared for, and communicated to, the OPSIM managers in the form of five different reports. These computer printouts include information about the results of operations of the period, by both variable costing and absorption costing, the financial position, the operating data not included in the above statements, and the industry financial data.

The first four statements supply the student with information which he uses to evaluate his decisions and to start planning for the future. The fifth report, the Industry Report, allows him to evaluate his decisions in comparison with the accomplishments of the other firms. Illustrations of typical reports the manager receives are presented in the last part of this chapter.

OPSIM Decision Making

OPSIM is an integrated operations management simulation. The management can consist of a single student or a team. The individual player will, of course, make all the firm's decisions. For team play, however (and it is anticipated that most circumstances will dictate team play), the division of decision-making should be spelled out to insure the participation of each team member. For the typical course in which it is utilized, the student is either nominally specialized or highly specialized. And in either case, there is little diversity in the basic decision-making knowledge of the students.

Consequently, the division of the decision-making process is not necessarily constrained to the usual functional areas. The following grouping of the responsibilities appears to be both highly practical and equitable. It is practical to the extent that the responsibility areas are grouped according to related decisions and efforts. It is equitable in that the workload for each student is approximately the same and the anticipated learning experiences are similarly distributed.

The participants for each firm should organize to make the current period's decisions. Organization should be encouraged. The selection of one of the managers as the chief executive officer of the firm might also be considered. The top executive should be responsible for integration of the specific decisions into the master plan. This position could be rotated each period so that each manager will have the experience of the overall aspect of decision making.

The responsibility divisions should also be rotated from time to time so that each manager will be exposed to varied organizational experiences. A more comprehensive discussion of this topic is presented in Chapter IV.

Possible responsibility divisions are:

1. Sales, including:

   a. forecasting demand for each product
   b. determining the optimum level of finished goods inventory
   c. determining the desired current production

2. Production, including:

   a. allocation of capacities
   b. scheduling of current production
   c. acquisition of raw materials
   d. acquisition of direct labor
   e. acquisition of maintenance labor

3. Capital budgeting, including:

   a. acquisition of new equipment

4. Finance, including:

   a. cash budgeting
   b. debt repayment
   c. investment in short-term securities
   d. sale of short-term securities

5. Budgeting and Analysis, including:

   a. preparation of *pro forma* statements
   b. analysis of actual performance.

Once the organization of the management of the firm has been completed, the task of decision making must be undertaken. Figure 3.1 shows the general inputs and requirements for OPSIM decisions.

To start the problem-solving process, *the student must review the environmental characteristics in Chapter II carefully. However, before proceeding he must then turn to the Accounting and Marketing Information Report* for the immediately past period *to obtain additional essential data.* For the first period's play this means that *the instructor must supply to the teams a copy of the test output* from his computer center.

Production Decisions: Typical Questions That Must Be Answered. Production management is not as simple as scheduling production for the current period alone. In many cases, product

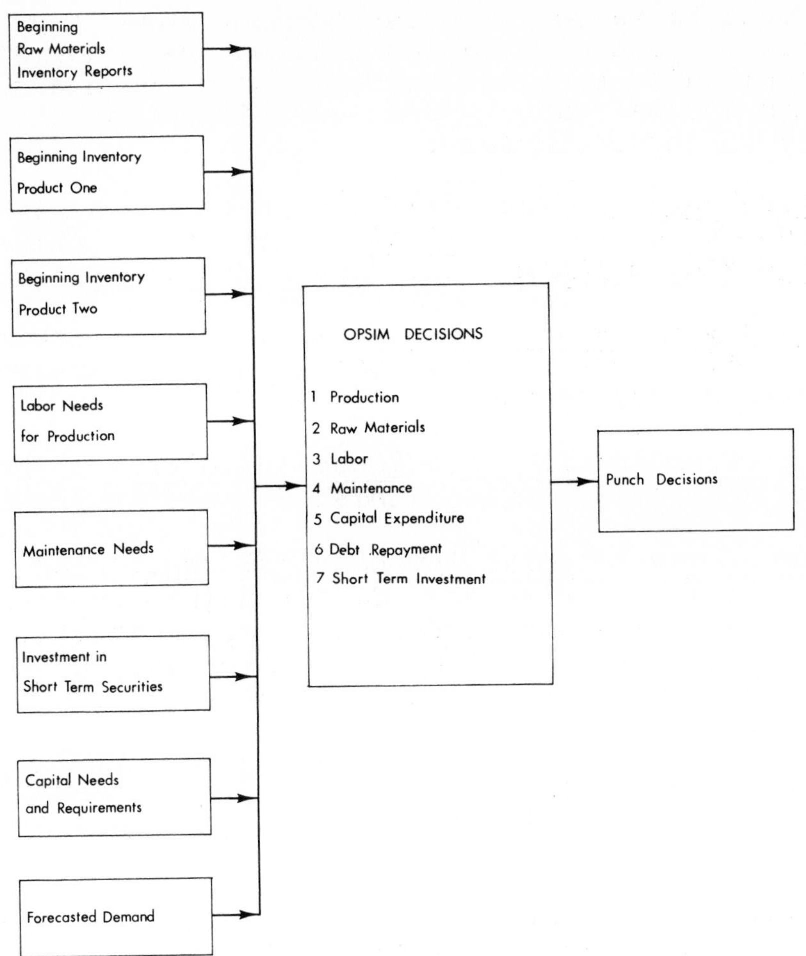

Figure 3-1. Inputs and Requirements for OPSIM Decisions.

inventories must be raised in order to meet some large demand in a future period. Such a situation implies that raw materials inventories should also be timed to facilitate the needed production increases and decreases. Some questions that the OPSIM manager must try to answer include:

1. Future demand: What will demand be for a given number of periods in the future? Predictions of demand form the bases for production scheduling and investment decisions.

2. Reliability of demand estimates: How reliable are the firm's demand estimates? This information is necessary in determining the size of safety stock.

3. Size of ending finished goods inventories: How large does the firm desire its ending finished goods inventories to be?

4. Size of raw material inventories: What size should ending raw material inventories be? Since ending inventories become next period's beginning inventories, and since management can use only raw materials out of beginning inventories, this question becomes most important for optimum production scheduling purposes.

5. Current production: Should the firm produce in the current period, and if so, what size lot should, and could, be produced?

The answers the student manager determines for these and other significant questions will ascertain the performance of his firm and, consequently, will reflect his decision-making ability.

Flow of the Decision-Making Process. To assist the student manager in his decision-making process, an integrated group of forms and schedules has been prepared which follows the logical flow of the decision-making process. This flow is basically as follows:

1. Forecast demand for Product One and Product Two.
2. Determine the desired level of finished goods inventories to be available for sale.
3. Compute the productive capabilities for the period, including the allocation of production capabilities between products.
4. Schedule the necessary production for the period.
5. Ascertain the utilization of the capacities.
6. Determine the raw materials required for production.
7. Compute the raw materials to be acquired.
8. Plan the direct labor hours required for production.
9. Select the maintenance labor hours to be acquired.

10. Determine the investment in capital goods (equipment).
11. Analyze the cash flow for the period, including debt repayment and purchase and sale of short-term securities.
12. Prepare pro forma statements for the period (specifically including budgeted contribution margin).
13. Analyze the actual results in comparison with the budgeted performance.

The schedules provided do not determine the values that the student manager should use; they are intended only to lead him through the decision-making process. The student must constantly refer to the description of the OPSIM environment during the decision-making process to determine relationships for managerial purposes.

Many students will want to expand their analysis to include speculation in the purchase of raw materials. Others may invest heavily in productive capacity or finished goods. How each student plays the game depends upon the strategy that his firm develops. To accomplish these objectives through objective analysis, the student will have to supplement the prepared schedules with his own creations. However, the values generated in these supplementary schedules should flow through the prepared schedules.

Management students may have to refer to the textbook in order to complete the various analyses. However, in general, the forms contain sufficient information to suggest specific analyses that may be used to determine acceptable alternatives. The student manager, however, should not be satisfied with only acceptable decisions and therefore should seek the best techniques available to utilize in his decision making. Appendix E gives a cross listing of leading textbooks and the various decision areas, supplying the latest techniques for solving managerial problems. The student should draw frequently from the texts.

A supply of blank schedules which the student should utilize in selecting the courses of action his firm will undertake during the periods of play are provided at the end of the manual. The forms include:

1. Input Decisions for the Period.

2. Sales Forecast.

3. Desired Current Production.

4. Scheduled Current Production.

5. Capacity Utilization.

6. Raw Materials Required for Production.

7. Raw Materials Acquisitions.

8. Direct Labor Required for Production.

9. Maintenance Labor Requirement.

10. Capital Expenditures.

11. Period Cost Budget.

12. Cash Budget.

13. Budgeted Contribution Margin and Period Contribution.

14. Analysis of Variance from Budgeted Contribution Margin and Net Income

Examples of OPSIM Decision Making. To orient the student in the use of the provided forms, selected examples of OPSIM decision making are given below. The examples include a brief discussion of the techniques that may be applied to specific decision areas. For those decision areas not illustrated, the student should draw upon his own knowledge and imagination in seeking optimum solutions. The prepared forms will, however, lead the student through the decision-making process and be of great assistance to him. Copies of all forms appear on pages 57-68.

Example 1:

The input decisions for the period's play are summarized on Form 1. Illustration 3.1 shows how Form 1 is to be utilized in reporting the following decisions: Production of 20,000 units of Product One and 15,000 units of Product Two; orders of raw materials 1, 2, and 3 of 25,000 pounds, 30,000 pounds and 31,000 pounds, respectively; contracting for 2,000 direct labor hours; hiring of 3 maintenance workers; purchase of 2 machines each for capacities one and two, 1 machine for capacity three and no change in capacity four; $50,000 in debt repaid; and, investment of $20,000 in short-term securities.

Example 2:

Sales forecasting is the most critical analysis undertaken by management. The answers obtained in this area are utilized by the manager in reaching decisions throughout the operations of the firm. Illustration 3.2 summarizes the sales forecast and the student should review the OPSIM environment to determine the behavioral patterns of the sales of each product. The values which

Illustration 3.1

Form 1

OPSIM Company 1

Firm No. 0 0 1
Columns 1 2 3

Input Decisions for the Period

Period 2

Period of Play 0 0 2
Columns 4 5 6

Decision Area		Decision Quantity
Production of Product One	Columns	0 0 2 0 0 0 0 7 8 9 10 11 12 13
Production of Product Two	Columns	0 0 1 5 0 0 0 14 15 16 17 18 19 20
Raw Material 1 Ordered	Columns	0 0 0 2 5 0 0 0 21 22 23 24 25 26 27 28
Raw Material 2 Ordered	Columns	0 0 0 3 0 0 0 0 29 30 31 32 33 34 35 36
Raw Material 3 Ordered	Columns	0 0 0 3 1 0 0 0 37 38 39 40 41 42 43 44
Direct Labor Hired	Columns	0 2 0 0 0 45 46 47 48 49
Maintenance Labor Hired	Columns	0 3 50 51
Investment in Capacity 1	Columns	0 2 52 53
Investment in Capacity 2	Columns	0 2 54 55
Investment in Capacity 3	Columns	0 2 56 57
Investment in Capacity 4	Columns	0 2 58 59
Debt Repayment	Columns	0 0 0 5 0 0 0 0 60 61 62 63 64 65 66 67
Purchase of ("-" Sale of Short-Term Securities	Columns	0 0 0 2 0 0 0 0 68 69 70 71 72 73 74 75
Administrator Penalties	Columns	76 77 78 79 80

Illustration 3.2

Form 2
OPSIM Company 1
Sales Forecast
Period 2

	Current Period Units	Current Period Dollars	Next Period Units
I. Product One			
1. Actual sales last period	16,000	1,200,000	
2. Estimated new orders			
a. Trend value	17,000		18,000
b. Seasonal value	2,000		1,500
c. Total new orders	19,000		19,500
3. Unfilled orders on hand	1,000		0
4. Gross estimated sales	20,000		19,500
5. Less lost sales			
a. Backorder cancellations	625		- 0
b. Stockout cancellations from other periods	0		313
c. Total lost sales	625		313
6. Total estimated sales	19,375	1,453,125	19,187
II. Product Two			
7. Actual sales last period	18,000		
8. Estimated new orders			
a. Trend value	19,000		21,000
b. Seasonal value	0		0
c. Total estimated new orders	19,000		21,000
9. Unfilled orders on hand	0		0
10. Gross estimated sales	19,000		21,000
11. Less estimated lost sales			
a. Stockout cancellations	0		0
b. Stockout cancellations from other periods	400		0
c. Total lost sales	400		0
12. Total estimated sales	18,600	1,209,000	21,000
III. Total Estimated Revenue			
13. a. Product One		$1,453,125	
b. Product Two		1,209,000	
c. Total		$2,662,125	

must be computed to derive demand for the period are shown in the illustration. Advanced students may evaluate the range of past values for further refinements of their answers. The new demand is always affected by previous stockouts; therefore, the net current demand will include values for backorders, backorder cancellations, and lost sales. Lost sales are the consequence in subsequent periods for stockouts in a previous period. Customers quit buying from the OPSIM firm if it cannot and does not fill their orders. The sales forecast must be made for two periods and the current period's demand is necessary in both units and dollars. These quantities are used to plan the current period's production and the current period's cash budget. The demand for next period, expressed only in units, is required so that the raw materials for that period can be ordered.

Example 3:

The desired current production analysis, as shown in Illustration 3.3, is determined by three factors: sales forecast, desired ending inventory, and inventory on hand.

Illustration 3.3

Form 3

OPSIM Company 1

Desired Current Production
Period 2

Item	Product One Quantity	Product Two Quantity
Sales Forecast (Units)	19,375	18,600
Plus: Desired Ending Inventory	5,000	4,000
Desired Goods Available	24,375	22,600
Less: Beginning Inventory	3,175	2600
Desired Current Production	21,200	20,000

The sales demand has already been computed on Form 2 and the inventory on hand is history. The determination of the desired ending inventory is the critical factor in this analysis. The goods demanded this period may be produced this period; therefore, the lead time is not a factor. The solution depends upon minimizing the sum of the carrying costs of holding excess finished goods and the opportunity cost of lost sales for not having sufficient finished goods available for sale. Advanced students should consider using stochastic models in determining the optimum solutions to this problem. In addition, the management of OPSIM may want to expand inventories of finished goods for cost reductions, minimizing setup costs, or speculating in future sales price or factor cost behavior.

Example 4:

The scheduled current production is determined by comparing the desired current production (computed on Form 3) with the productive capacity available. The lower of the two values constitutes the current production scheduled for the period. For example, Illustration 3.4 shows that desired current production is 20,000 units and that productive capacity available is 15,000 units. Therefore, the OPSIM firm schedules production of 15,000 units because that is the maximum amount that it can produce. On the other hand, if in the above example the productive capacity were 25,000 units, the firm would produce only 20,000 units because that quantity is all that it desires.

The primary problem in determining the scheduled current production is the computation of the productive capacity available. In OPSIM, the firm produces two products that compete for the productive capacities. The student manager must, therefore, solve the allocation problem before he can determine the productive capacity available for each product. The graphical, linear programming analysis is ideal for this purpose. Some technique of this sort must be used when the joint demand for productive capacities exceeds the available capacities.

Example 5:

The flow of raw materials to the OPSIM manager is especially important. The primary characteristic of this flow is a one-period delay between ordering and utilization. Raw material requirements for the next period must be planned for this period. This analysis is further complicated by the fact that the current period's utilization of existing inventories of raw materials will affect the decisions for the next period. Illustration 3.5 gives an example of the raw materials acquisition budget.

The OPSIM manager may desire to hold quantities of raw materials in excess of the production and safety stock requirements. Therefore, the new data introduced in this form is the desired ending inventory levels. By pursuing different strategies, the different OPSIM managers arrive at different answers to this problem.

Illustration 3.4

Form 4

OPSIM Company 1

Scheduled Current Production
Period 2

Item	Product One Quantity	Product Two Quantity
Desired Current Production	21,200	20,000
Allocated Production Capacity Available	20,000	21,000
Scheduled Current Production	20,000	20,000

Reporting

The efforts and accomplishments of a particular period of activity for a business entity are summarized in the financial statements covering that period. The net results of these activities are compared to the resources employed by the firm to evaluate its progress during the period. Financial statements, as conventionally prepared, are intended as general purpose statements and, consequently, only present data in summarized form. For stockholders, potential investors, general public, and regulatory governmental agencies, the content of the statements is generally accepted as adequate. For managerial purposes, the financial data presented is inadequate.

Management must, of course, be interested in the reported profits or losses for the period. However, the decision maker is even more interested in the individual causes of those items conglomerated to produce the reported profit or loss. Management

Illustration 3.5

Form 7
OPSIM Company 1

Raw Materials Acquisitions
Period 2

Item		Raw Materials					
		1		2		3	
Estimated Production Next Period		Conversion Rate	Units	Conversion Rate	Units	Conversion Rate	Units
Product	Quantity						
1	19,000			40	760,000	10	190,000
2	22,000	25	550,000			15	330,000
Estimated Requirement for Next Period			550 000		760,000		520,000
Plus Estimated Desired Ending Inventory Next Period			50,000		60,000		80,000
Requirement Next Period			600,000		820,000		600,000
Plus Current Production Requirements			500,000		800,000		500,000
Total Requirement			1,100,000		1,620,000		1,100,000
Less Inventory on Hand			700,000		900,000		550,000
Units to be acquired this period			400,000		720,000		550,000
Unit Cost			1.00		.50		1.50
Total Cost			400,000		360,000		825,000

must further attempt to identify those items which are controllable and those items which are not controllable. The adage that all costs are controllable in the long run is not adequate since operational decisions must be made in the short run. Managerial decisions are made in given environments and some of the environmental factors change as a consequence of decisions and others do not. Those factors which change as a result of managerial decision making are termed "controllable." Some factors can not be controlled by management, and, as such, are irrelevant for decision-making purposes.

The area constituted by the controllable factors encompasses the area of managerial decision making, and these items may be caused to increase or decrease through specific actions. The consequence of such changes is of vital interest to management for planning and controlling. Basically, management needs, in addition to the conventional financial statements, specialized statements which supply it with the behavior of the controllable financial data. Also, it needs reports covering some nonfinancial items which are necessary in the decision-making process. Data concerning the industry as a whole allow the OPSIM manager to evaluate his performance in the light of the performances of the other OPSIM managers.

The completion of the decision forms and schedules for a particular period of OPSIM is the culmination of comprehensive planning of the operation of the firm by the participant. Such a process closely parallels the decision-making process of real business firms. OPSIM executes the decisions made by the student (within the constraints of the environment) and then presents the results of these courses of action in a series of reports. These statements have been designed to provide data to facilitate the evaluation of the benefit or the detriment of those decisions to the firm, and to provide pertinent data for subsequent decision-making activities.

Specifically, these reports consist of the following statements:

1. <u>The Managerial Operations Statement</u>, which presents in detail the controllable areas of the firm's operations along with the totals of the non-controllable items.

2. <u>The Current Balance Sheet</u>, which presents the resources and their sources in conventional accounting form after the results of the operations for each given period.

3. <u>The Conventional Income Statement</u>, which reports the results of operations on the absorption basis.

4. <u>The Accounting and Marketing Information Report</u>, which

contains relevant data not reported in the other statements.

5. The Industry Report, which reports the marginal contribution and net income for the current period for each OPSIM firm along with the total equity of each firm as of that date.

Managerial Operations Statement. The primary purpose of the Managerial Operations Statement is to provide management with financial data arranged according to its controllable and non-controllable nature. In OPSIM the classifications used to fulfill this objective are sales, variable cost, and period cost. The first two classifications are given in total and by product, while the latter item, which constitutes all other costs which do not vary directly with the decisions made, is given in unallocated totals.

The computer output of the management operations statement, as shown in Illustration 3.6, is prepared each period for each team, with each team's number and period designated on the top left-hand corner of the statement.

The content of the Managerial Operations Statement is arranged by those accounts which can be associated with either Product One or Product Two. After the individual product figures have been presented, the overall totals for each item are then shown. At the bottom of the statement, those accounts, which are period costs and not identifiable with either product, are presented.

Specifically, the items appearing in the statement are as follows:

1. Sales is found by multiplying the sales price of each respective product times the quantity of that product sold. In the first column the total sales for Product One is presented. The sales for Product Two appears in the second column, while the total sales of Product One and Product Two are accumulated in the third column and constitute the total sales of the firm for the period.

2. Other income is the total earnings on short-term securities. For OPSIM purposes, the earnings on short-term securities are included in the operating revenue. The justification for this classification is that these earnings reflect decision-making policies of operating management.

3. Total revenue is the sum of sales and other income.

4. Cost of goods sold is the variable cost of those items sold during the period. The cost flow utilized in determining this amount is the first in - first out (FIFO) method.

Illustration 3.6

OPERATIONS MANAGEMENT SIMULATICN

PERIOD 1

MANAGERIAL OPERATIONS STATEMENT

FIRM 1

	UNITS	PRODUCT ONE	PRODUCT TWO	TOTALS
SALES		1261500.	1238900.	2500400.
OTHER INCOME				-0.
TOTAL INCOME				2500400.
LESS VARIABLE COST OF GOODS SOLD				
BEGINNING INVENTORY-FINISHED GOODS		565520.	808000.	1373520.
CURRENT PRODUCTION				
DIRECT LABOR		18900.	9000.	27900.
DIRECT MATERIALS				
RAW MATERIALS ONE USED	250000.		250000.	250000.
RAW MATERIALS TWO USED	600000.	300000.		300000.
RAW MATERIALS THREE USED	300000.	225000.	225000.	450000.
TOTAL CIRECT MATERIALS COST				1000000.
VARIABLE OVERHEAD		1050.	500.	1550.
COST OF CURRENT PRODUCTICN(VAR)		544950.	484500.	1029450.
TOTAL GCOCS AVAILABLE		1110470.	1292500.	2402970.
LESS ENDING INVENTORY		550938.	522476.	1073414.
VARIABLE COST OF GOODS SOLD		559532.	770024.	1329556.
VARIABLE PRODUCTION MARGIN		701968.	468876.	1170844.
LESS ADDITICNAL PERIOD COSTS				
SELLING ANC ADMIN. EXPENSES				503704.
OVERHEAD				384000.
INTEREST				-0.
ADDITIONAL PERIOD COSTS				887704.
CCNTRIBUTION FRCM OPERATICNS				283139.

Specifically, however, all goods produced during the period are assigned the same cost, computed by aggregating all variable product costs and dividing by the quantity produced during the period. Current sales are first supplied out of beginning inventory, (at the unit cost of beginning inventory), and when orders exceed beginning inventory, the excess is supplied out of current production (at the unit cost of current production). At the end of the period the unit cost of those products still on hand is determined by dividing the total units on hand into the total cost of the ending inventory.

The elements involved in computing the cost of goods sold are as follows:

5. Finished goods beginning inventory is the variable cost of those products on hand at the beginning of the period.

6. Current production is the sum of the variable cost incurred during the period in the production of the specific products. All units started during the period are assumed to be completed. Therefore, no process inventories exist at either the beginning or the ending of the play. Those variable costs included in the current production are:

a. Direct Labor is the total cost of the production workers during the period employed in the production of each respective product. If more labor is hired than is utilized in production, the excess is charged to the period costs.

b. Direct Materials is the total of the three raw materials which are used in the production. Raw materials are accounted for on a perpetual basis and are costed into production on the same basis as finished goods, i.e., modified FIFO. Illustration 3.6 shows that the raw materials used are assigned only to the production of the particular product involved. For instance:

(1) Raw Material 1 is used only in the production of Product Two, so the total cost of raw material 1 used is the same total as the cost of raw material 1 used for Product Two.

(2) Raw Material 2 is utilized only in Product One, so the total cost of this item is equal to the Product One cost.

(3) Raw Material 3 is employed in the production of both products and the cost for each is determined by the units used

in the production of the respective products.

(4) The total direct materials cost for the period has been presented in the total column, and is the sum of the costs of raw materials 1, 2, and 3.

7. Variable Overhead is the total of all other variable costs of producing the products. Depreciation and other fixed costs are specifically eliminated from the cost of current production. This cost per product is determined by the hours of utilization of each of the respective types of production machinery.

The cost of current production is then totaled for each product with the grand total accumulated in the total column.

8. Total Goods Available is the variable cost of beginning inventory and current production and is shown for each product, as well as the total.

9. Ending Inventory is the residual balance left over in determining the cost of goods sold on a perpetual basis. It, also, is shown for the individual products and in total. Variable cost of goods sold is determined by first costing all goods sold at the unit cost of beginning inventories with the remaining units sold costed at the average cost of current production per unit.

10. Variable Production Margin plus "other income" equals the contribution margin in total for each product, and is then determined for the company as a whole, including the earnings on short-term securities. It is computed by subtracting the variable cost of goods sold from the sales revenue of each product, then accumulating these to determine the total contribution margin.

11. Additional Period Costs include all other outlays made during the period by the firm that do not constitute a product cost. Since they cannot be identified with any particular product, they are therefore taken directly to the totals column. Included as period costs are selling and administrative expenses, other overhead expenses, and interest expense. The selling and administrative expenses are those items associated with marketing the products of the firm and conducting the general affairs of the business. These are the corporate salaries, the cost of carrying finished goods, and the marketing costs. The overhead expenses consist of all of the costs of manufacturing not included in the variable cost of production. Specifically, it includes the plant period costs, the carrying costs and ordering costs of raw materials, the product setup

cost for both products, along with the maintenance costs for the period and the excess direct labor cost.

The period contribution from operations is the net figure obtained by subtracting the period cost from the production margin. From the managerial standpoint, it constitutes the overall net contribution to the firm from all activities during the period.

Balance Sheet.

Each period the teams are provided with a current balance sheet showing the results of operations. Illustration 3.7 is a typical example of that statement. The date of the balance sheet is always printed on the statement in the top left-hand corner to identify the last period included in the statement. Similarly, the team number is printed in the same location. The balance sheet presented is similar to the conventional one prepared for businesses. For OPSIM, some items have been combined as the separate amounts were not relevant for management purposes. Those items appearing on a balance sheet are as follows:

1. Current Assets. Current assets are those items commonly identified as the working capital of the firm, *i.e.*, those items which circulate to generate profits for the business. Included in the OPSIM current assets are:

a. Cash on hand at the end of the period.

b. Short-term Securities--temporary investment of short-run excess cash.

c. Accounts Receivable due from customers from the sale of Products One and Two with no experience of losses from such accounts.

d. Inventories of both finished goods and direct materials, which are carried at weighted-average (modified FIFO) absorption cost:

(1) Finished goods on hand at the end of the period consist of the absorption cost of producing the units of both Produst One and Product Two still on hand at the end of the period. These amounts are presented separately for each product and are added together to produce the total cost of finished goods on hand.

Illustration 3.7

PERIOD 1 BALANCE SHEET

FIRM 1

ASSETS			LIABILITIES	
CURRENT ASSETS			DEBT	-0.
CASH		143126.		
ACCOUNTS RECEIVABLE		750120.	OWNERS EQUITY	5013896.
SHORT TERM SECURITIES		-0.		
INVENTORY				
FINISHED GOODS				
PRODUCT ONE	785247.			
PRODUCT TWO	680403.			
TOTAL		1465650.		
RAW MATERIALS				
MATERIALS ONE	760000.			
MATERIAL TWO	305000.			
MATERIAL THREE	600000.			
TOTAL		1665000.		
PLANT AND EQUIPMENT		990000.		
TOTAL ASSETS		5013896.	TOTAL LIABILITIES AND EQUITY	5013896.

(2) Direct materials consist of the cost of acquiring those raw materials available at the end of the period. The cost of each raw material on hand is shown separately. They are combined to present the total raw material inventory amount.

2. Plant and Equipment. Plant and equipment includes land, plant, and machinery. For the OPSIM learning experience, no benefit would be derived by presenting these separately. The periodic depreciation taken on those depreciable items has been netted against the cost, thereby resulting in the book value being presented on the balance sheet. Depreciation is computed on the straight line basis and amounts to $5,000 per period for the plant and $1500, $1000, $1500, and $1000 for each item of machinery 1, 2, 3, and 4, respectively.

3. Total Assets. Total assets is the sum of the current assets and plant and equipment items.

4. Liabilities. The only liabilities of the firm are its commitments on an open line of credit from a financial institution which charges 2% interest per period for balances outstanding at the end of the period.

5. Capital. All the capital of the business has been grouped under one account simply called owner's equity. In this account are the accumulation of the owner's original contributions plus all the profits or losses accumulated to date. OPSIM companies are operated as growth companies and have a policy of no dividend payments.

The absorption Income Statement. The absorption income statement is prepared, basically, according to conventional accounting principles. It is only indirectly useful to management, and it is included primarily so that the OPSIM management will be aware of the operating results as reported to outsiders.

Illustration 3.8 represents a typical absorption income statement. The classification used in it basically follows that of the managerial operations statement. The primary difference is that those period costs related to production have been allocated to the current period's production. The factor used to allocate these costs is the machine hours used in the production of the two products.

The inventory amounts as well as the cost of goods sold is stated as the total cost on an absorption basis. Total operating expenses and other expenses have been added together to reduce redundant subtotals. The net profit is thus determined directly from gross profit.

Illustration 3.8

PERIOD 1 ABSORPTION INCOME STATEMENT

FIRM 1

	PRODUCT CNE	PRODUCT TWO	TOTALS
SALES	1261500.	1238900.	2500400.
OTHER INCOME			-0.
TOTAL INCOME			2500400.
LESS COST OF GOODS SOLD			
BEGINNING INVENTORY-FINISHED GOODS	935000.	900000.	1835000.
CURRENT PRODUCTION			
DIRECT LABOR	18900.	9000.	27900.
DIRECT MATERIALS			
RAW MATERIALS ONE		250000.	250000.
RAW MATERIALS TWO	300000.		300000.
RAW MATERIALS THREE	225000.	225000.	450000.
VARIABLE OVERHEAD	1050.	500.	1550.
OTHER ALLOCATED OVERHEAD	230397.	153603.	384000.
COST OF CURRENT PRODUCTION	775347.	638103.	1413450.
GOODS AVAILABLE FOR SALE	1710347.	1538103.	3248450.
LESS ENDING INVENTORY	785247.	680403.	1465650.
COST OF GOODS SOLD	925100.	857700.	1782800.
PRODUCTION CONTRIBUTION	336400.	381200.	717600.
OPERATING EXPENSES			
MARKETING AND ADMIN. EXPENSES			503704.
INTEREST PAYMENTS			-0.
TOTAL OPERATING EXPENSES			503704.
PROFIT BEFORE TAXES			213896.

Accounting and Marketing Information Report. There are several types of information that do not appear on the previous statements that management should know about. To obtain information of the most important of these factors, OPSIM prepares a general accounting and marketing information report. Illustration 3.9 is a typical example of this report.

The report contains the following information:

1. Finished Goods Inventories. The data provided encompass the total unit flow for both Product One and Product Two from the beginning inventory to the ending inventory.

2. Raw Materials Inventories. The analysis and planning associated with raw materials are critical. This primarily results from the one period delay between the requisition and the subsequent availability of these items. The data concerning raw material units contained in this section therefore are arranged so that the ending inventory is the usable balance for the subsequent period.

3. Carrying Costs. This information is useful in controlling both overhead and operating expenses. The carrying costs relate to both finished goods by product and raw materials by type. The amount cited is for a single unit of the inventory item for the next period only.

4. Setup and Ordering Cost. The nature of these costs has already been described in Chapter II. These costs are segregated from other cumulative cost figure in order that the OPSIM manager may control inventory expense and more efficiently plan future inventory levels. Every production effort requires setup cost. If no production for a particular product is scheduled then no setup cost is incurred. Both the setup costs and the ordering costs for raw materials have been set at levels which require carful analysis in these activities in order to select the optimum course of action.

5. Unit Prices. The market research department of the OPSIM companies supplies to the firm management the actual unit prices for both the finished goods and the raw materials. For the finished goods the sales prices per unit are supplied for both products for the next period. Initially, these prices for Product One and Product Two are $75 and $65 per unit, respectively; however, the game administrator is free to change these prices for the entire industry through changes on the finger tip parameter card. Notice of changes in the price structure should be given by the administrator two periods in advance. The team players may find it convenient to think of the price structure of the OPSIM industry as pure competition. Changes in the relationship between the prices of the two products may result in changes in their production mix. These changes may also affect

Illustration 3.9

ACCOUNTING INFORMATION (PHYSICAL UNITS)

FIRM 1

FINISHED GOODS INVENTORIES

	PRODUCT ONE	PRODUCT TWO
BEGINNING INVENTORY	17000.	20000.
PLUS CURRENT PRODUCTION	15000.	10000.
GOODS AVAILABLE FOR SALE	32000.	30000.
LESS CURRENT SALES	16820.	19060.
ENDING INVENTORY	15180.	10940.
CARRYING COST	3218.	2321.
SETUP COST	5000.	6000.
UNIT PRICE PERIOD 1	75.	65.
PRODUCT DEMAND PERIOD 1	16820.	19060.
PRODUCT DEMAND PERIOD 2.	17080.	20580.
PRODUCT DEMAND PERIOD 3.	18180.	21180.

RAW MATERIALS INVENTORIES

	MATERIAL ONE	MATERIAL TWO	MATERIAL THREE
BEGINNING INVENTORY	510000.	610000.	300000.
LESS MATERIALS USED	250000.	600000.	300000.
UNUSED MATERIALS	260000.	10000.	-0.
PLUS CURRENT ORDERS	500000.	600000.	400000.
ENDING INVENTORY	760000.	610000.	400000.
	38500.	34100.	13500.
	1500.	2000.	2000.
	1.00	0.50	1.50

the desired inventory levels of both products.

The cost per unit of each of the raw materials is given only for the current period. The student is expected to analyze carefully the behavior of the cost of the raw material and from this analysis, the firm must determine its raw materials inventory levels.

6. Product Demand. The forecasting of the product demand by the research department is limited. Only an attempt at determining the basic long-run behavior of the product demand can be made. Therefore, these estimates for subsequent periods should be adjusted by any special behavior that the firm's management deduces--such as seasonal effects. The actual demand for each product is presented for the current period just completed plus the estimated demand for the next two periods.

The Industry Report.

So that the managers of the OPSIM firm may compare their overall performance with that of the managers of competing firms, an industry report is prepared after each period of play. The results of each team's efforts are summarized by: (1) the contribution margin for the current period; (2) the profit for the current period; and (3) the equity balance at the end of the current period. A typical industry report is as shown in Illustration 3.10.

Summary.

OPSIM decision-making is designed to simulate its real-world counterpart in operations management. The ability of the OPSIM manager to choose the optimum courses of action in the several decision areas is reflected in the profits that his firm accumulates.

To select the optimum alternatives the student manager must acquire a thorough knowledge of the environment in which he operates. The student should carefully review Chapter II for relevant aspects of the environment.

A sound knowledge of the "facts of the situation" allows the game participant to draw upon the best techniques available to him in analyzing the environment. Specifically, the OPSIM manager can employ several operations research techniques in evaluating the various alternatives. To assist the student in his decision-making process, OPSIM provides an integrated series of forms. These forms include all of the decision areas and also

Illustration 3.10

INDUSTRY REPORT

	CONTRIBUTION	EQUITY	PROFIT
TEAM 1	283139.	5013896.	213896.
TEAM 2	264713.	5006417.	206417.
TEAM 3	307435.	5020678.	220678.
TEAM 4	301331.	5026842.	226842.
TEAM 5	300326.	5022140.	222140.
TEAM 6	283139.	5013896.	213896.
TEAM 7	301409.	5026868.	226868.
TEAM 8	283139.	5013896.	213896.
TEAM 9	294983.	5026965.	226965.
TEAM10	258374.	5007041.	207041.

provide for a master budget of both contribution margin and period contribution.

The student should utilize the forms in making each period's decisions. In doing this, he integrates the specific decisions into a master operating plan. Consequently, each course of action selected is evaluated in the light of the total plans for the period.

After the necessary decisions for a given period have been made and have been processed by the computer, five different reports are prepared for each OPSIM firm. These reports are to be utilized by the management in evaluating their decisions. The managerial operations statement isolates the controllable factors from the non-controllable. Therefore, it becomes the most important statement for management.

Other financial statements include the income statement (using absorption costing) and the balance sheet. There are some data needed by the decision-maker which are not included in the above statements. These data are basically internal operating items and are presented in the special accounting and marketing information report.

For the student to evaluate his decision-making ability, an industry report is supplied each period. It contains the current period's contribution margin and income for all OPSIM firms, as well as the total equity accumulated over the life of the game to date for each firm. Here, the student can see his relative standing in the industry. Specifically, the student should utilize form 14 to evaluate his planned results against his actual results. By so doing, he can identify areas in which variances occur. These "variance" become the topics for more detailed evaluation in future planning.

Form 1

OPSIM Company ___ Firm No. ___ ___ ___
Columns 1 2 3

Input Decisions for the Period

Period ___ Period of Play ___ ___ ___
Columns 4 5 6

Decision Area		Decision Quantity
Production of Product One	Columns	7 8 9 10 11 12 13
Production of Product Two	Columns	14 15 16 17 18 19 20
Raw Material 1 Ordered	Columns	21 22 23 24 25 26 27 28
Raw Material 2 Ordered	Columns	29 30 31 32 33 34 35 36
Raw Material 3 Ordered	Columns	37 38 39 40 41 42 43 44
Direct Labor Hired	Columns	45 46 47 48 49
Maintenance Labor Hired	Columns	50 51
Investment in Capacity 1	Columns	52 53
Investment in Capacity 2	Columns	54 55
Investment in Capacity 3	Columns	56 57
Investment in Capacity 4	Columns	58 59
Debt Repayment	Columns	60 61 62 63 64 65 66 67
Purchase or (-) Sale of Short-Term Securities	Columns	68 69 70 71 72 73 74 75
Administrator Penalties	Columns	76 77 78 79 80

Form 2
OPSIM Company ___
Sales Forecast ___
Period ___

	Current Period Units	Current Period Dollars	Next Period Units
I. Product One			
1. Actual sales last period	___	___	___
2. Estimated new orders			
a. Trend value	___	___	___
b. Seasonal value	___	___	___
c. Total new orders	___	___	___
3. Unfilled orders on hand	___	___	___
4. Gross estimated sales	___	___	___
5. Less lost sales			
a. Backorder cancellations	___	___	___
b. Stockout cancellations from other periods	___	___	___
c. Total lost sales	___	___	___
6. Total estimated sales	___	___	___
II. Product Two			
7. Actual sales last period	___	___	___
8. Estimated new orders			
a. Trend value	___	___	___
b. Seasonal value	___	___	___
c. Total estimated new orders	___	___	___
9. Unfilled orders on hand	___	___	___
10. Gross estimated sales	___	___	___
11. Less estimated lost sales			
a. Stockout cancellations	___	___	___
b. Stockout cancellations from other periods	___	___	___
c. Total lost sales	___	___	___
12. Total estimated sales	___	___	___
III. Total Estimated Revenue			
13. a. Product One		___	
b. Product Two		___	
c. Total		___	

Form 3
OPSIM Company ___
Desired Current Production
Period ___

Description	Product One	Product Two
Sales Forecast	___	___
Plus Desired Ending Inventory	___	___
Desired Goods Available For Sale	___	___
Less Beginning Inventory	___	___
Desired Current Production	___	___

Form 4
OPSIM Company ___
Scheduled Current Production
Period ___

Description	Product One	Product Two
Desired Current Production	___	___
Allocated Production Capacity Available	___	___
Scheduled Current Production	___	___

Form 5
OPSIM Company ___
Capacity Utilization and Variable Overhead Cost
Period ___

Description	Capacities 1	2	3	4
Current Capacity:				
Number of Machines				
Hours of Capacity Per Machine				
Capacity Hours Available				
Less Capacity Required for Current Production:				
Product One:				
Production Scheduled				
Conversion Rate				
Total Hours Required				
Capacity Hours Available for Product Two:				
Less Product Two:				
Production Scheduled				
Conversion Rate				
Total Hours Required				
Excess Capacity				
Capacity Hours Available				
Less Excess Capacity				
Capacity Utilized				
Variable Overhead Rate				
Total Variable Overhead				
Less Variable Overhead Product One				
Variable Overhead Product Two				

Form 6
OPSIM Company ___
Raw Materials Required For Production
Period ___

Current Production		Raw Materials					
		1		2		3	
Product	Quantity	Conversion Rate	Units Required	Conversion Rate	Units Required	Conversion Rate	Units Required
1							
2							
Raw Materials Required							
Unit Cost							
Total Raw Material Cost							
Raw Material Cost:							
Product One							
Product Two							

Form 7
OPSIM Company ___
Raw Materials Acquisitions
Period ___

Item		Raw Materials					
		1		2		3	
Estimated Production Next Period		Conversion Rate	Units	Conversion Rate	Units	Conversion Rate	Units
Product	Quantity	___	___	___	___	___	___
1	___	___	___	___	___	___	___
2	___	___	___	___	___	___	___
Estimated Requirement for Next Period			___		___		___
Plus Estimated Desired Ending Inventory Next Period			___		___		___
Requirement Next Period			___		___		___
Plus Current Production Requirements			___		___		___
Total Requirement			___		___		___
Less Inventory on Hand			___		___		___
Units to be acquired this period			___		___		___
Unit Cost			___		___		___
Total Cost			═══		═══		═══

Form 8
OPSIM Company ___
Direct Labor Required For Production Schedule
Period ___

Current Production		Direct Labor Hours			
Product	Quantity	Conversion Rate	Hours Required	Hourly Cost	Total Cost
1					
2					
Total Labor Required					

Form 9
OPSIM Company ___
Maintenance Labor Hired
Period ___

Description	Quantity
Maintenance Workers	
Pay Rate	
Total Cost	

Form 10
OPSIM Company ___
Capital Expenditures
Period ___

Item	Quantity	Unit Cost	Total Cost
Machine 1	______	______	______
Machine 2	______	______	______
Machine 3	______	______	______
Machine 4	______	______	______
Total Capital Expenditures			______

Form 11
OPSIM Company ___
Period Cost Budget
Period ___

				Cost
Cash Expenses:				
Carrying Costs:				
	Average Inventory	Rate	Cost	
Product One	___	___	___	
Product Two	___	___	___	
Raw Material 1	___	___	___	
Raw Material 2	___	___	___	
Raw Material 3	___	___	___	$___
Setup Costs:				
Product One			___	
Product Two			___	___
Ordering Costs:				
Raw Material 1			___	
Raw Material 2			___	
Raw Material 3			___	___
Fixed Production Costs (Excluding Depreciation)				___
Selling and Administrative Cost				___
Interest Expense				___
Total Cash Costs for the Period				___
Depreciation Expenses:				
	Number of Machines	Periodic Charge	Amount	
C1	___	___	___	
C2	___	___	___	
C3	___	___	___	
C4	___	___	___	
Plant	___	___	___	
Total Period Cost			___	___
				═══

Form 12
OPSIM Company ___
Cash Budget
Period ___

Description				Amount
Cash on Hand				
Plus: Cash from Operations:	Amount	Per Cent Collected This Period	Received	
Current Sales	___	___	___	
Collection of last Period's Receivables	___	___	___	
Interest Income	___	___	___	___
Cash Available				___
Less: Cash for Operations:				
Variable Overhead		Amount		
Product One		___		
Product Two		___	___	
Raw Materials Purchases				
One		___		
Two		___		
Three		___	___	
Direct Labor			___	
Maintenance Labor			___	
Period Costs			___	___
Net Cash Balance from Operations				___
Plus: Cash From Sale of Short-Term Securities				___
Adjusted Cash				___
Plus: Debt Acquired (only if overdrawn)				___
Available Cash				___
Less: Debt Repayment				___
Excess Cash				___
Less: Purchase of Short-term securities				___
Ending Cash Balance				___

Form 13
OPSIM Company ___
Budgeted Contribution Margin and Period Contribution
Period ___

Description	Product One Amount	Product Two Amount	Total
Sales	___	___	___
Less Variable Cost of Goods Sold:			
Beginning Inventory	___	___	___
Cost of Current Production:			
RM1	___	___	___
RM2	___	___	___
RM3	___	___	___
Direct Labor	___	___	___
Variable Overhead			
Cost of Production	___	___	___
Cost of Goods Available	___	___	___
Less Ending Inventory	___	___	___
Cost of Goods Sold	___	___	___
Contribution Margin	___	___	___
Period Contribution	___	___	___

Form 14
OPSIM Company ___
Analysis of Variances from Budgeted Contribution Margin
Period ___

	Product One	Product Two	Total
Actual Contribution Margin	______	______	______
Budgeted Contribution Margin	______	______	______
Variance From Budget (Unfavorable)	======	======	======
<u>Volume Variance</u>			
Budgeted Sales in Units	______	______	
Actual Sales in Units	______	______	
Volume Variance in Units	______	______	
Revenue Variance:			
Budgeted Sales Price Per Unit	______	______	
Revenue Variance (Sales Price times Volume Variance)	______	______	
Cost Variance:			
Budgeted Cost Per Unit	______	______	
Cost Variance (Cost Times Volume Variance)	______	______	______
Volume Variance	======	======	======
<u>Cost Variance</u>			
Actual Sales in Units	______	______	
Budgeted Unit Cost	______	______	
Budgeted Variable Cost	______	______	
Actual Variable Cost	______	______	
Cost Variance	______	______	______
Total Contribution Margin Variance	======	======	======

CHAPTER IV

OPSIM GAME INSTRUCTIONS AND INFORMATION

In order to use the _Operations Management Simulation_ optimally, both students and instructor must learn some basic procedures. Neither group, however, must understand the computer program in which the environment is contained, nor any of the technical aspects of OPSIM. All that is required is a campus computer center, an initial set of card decks, and a basic understanding of how to punch decision cards (this can be done by the students prior to submitting decision). The initial card decks will be mailed to the instructor upon adoption of the _Operations Management Simulation_.

The following pages are designed to provide answers to these questions: (1) What are the basic steps involved in playing the _Operations Management Simulation_? (2) How are the decisions _punched on data cards_? (3) What kinds of reports does the simulation produce for planning and decision making purposes? and (4) What steps are involved in "setting up" to run OPSIM? Careful study of this material allows the participants to proceed with the _Operations Management Simulation_ with an air of confidence.

A General Approach to Game Play.

Figure 4.1 illustrates the basic steps that are involved in administrating and playing the _Operations Management Simulation_. First, each student firm must make decisions, which are facilitated by the use of the decision forms at the ends of Chapters II and III. These decisions are then punched on data cards. The formats showing how, and where, to punch each decision on the appropriate data card are illustrated in another section of this chapter.

Once the decision cards have been punched, the game administrator performs the following routine: first, the decision cards are collected; second, the decision cards are "arranged" by firm number, with the decision of firm one at the top of the deck followed by the decision cards of the other firms; third, the history deck is replaced by a new history deck, which is the punched output from last period's play; fourth, the decision cards are now placed behind the history deck.

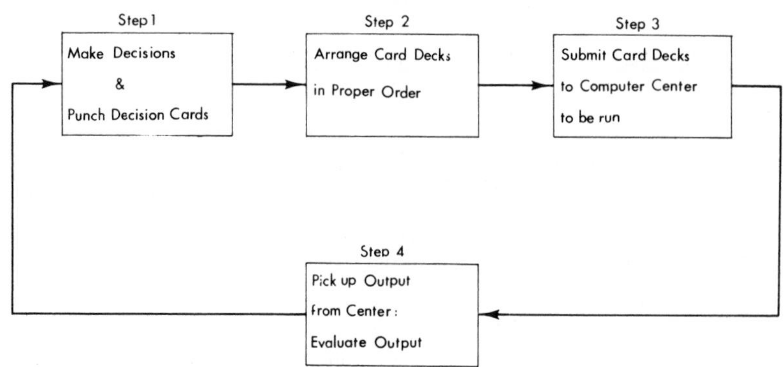

Figure 4-1. The Basic Steps Involved in Playing the Decision Making Game.

The third step is to take the newly arranged deck to the computer center. At this point, a computer center technician can add the appropriate control cards and run the program. The instructor may assign a grader to perform all of these routine tasks.

The final step is to pick up the printed output, <u>and the newly punched history cards</u>. The newly punched history cards are to replace the old history cards on the next computer run. Note that the "old" history here is the "new" history discussed in the routine of step two. The printed output is the various reports and statements needed for evaluating decisions as compared to competitors. These reports also form the basis for future planning and control of the production operations, and the game process just described begins anew.

<u>OPSIM Decisions: Inputs and Punching</u>.

In order to make decisions in any period, the management of an OPSIM firm needs information about the company's present position and the nature of future demand. Figure 4.2 illustrates the inputs necessary to make decisions. The pivot point for any production scheduling is the acquisition of a reliable sales forecast. The student <u>must</u> forecast, even with the small amount

DECISION AREA	UNIT OF ACCOUNT	DECISION FIELD COLUMNS
Production of Product 1	Products	7-13
Production of Product 2	Products	14-20
Raw Material 1 Ordered	Units	21-28
Raw Material 2 Ordered	Units	29-36
Raw Material 3 Ordered	Units	37-44
Direct Labor Hired	Hours	45-49
Maintenance Labor Hired	Number of Workers	50-51
Investment in Capacity 1	Number of Machines	52-53
Investment in Capacity 2	Number of Machines	54-55
Investment in Capacity 3	Number of Machines	56-57
Investment in Capacity 4	Number of Machines	58-59
Debt Repayment	Dollars	60-67
Investment in Short-Term Securities	Dollars	68-75
Administrator's Penalty	Dollars	76-80

Figure 4.2. Unit of Account and Field Lengths for Each Type of Decision.

of information at his disposal.

How the Administrator "Sets Up" for OPSIM Play.

A few preliminaries must be carried out before the administrator can confidently launch OPSIM play. First, the initial card decks and this manual must be acquired from the publisher. When the card decks are received, the administrator should arrange the four decks in the order shown in Figure 4.3. In turn, behind the source deck is placed the parameter card, the history deck, and the decision deck.

The Parameter Card. The parameter card follows the source deck (usually the computer center will insert a control card between the two decks) and remains in this position throughout the game play. While the history and decision decks are replaced from period to period, the parameter card is not replaced and should not be disturbed after play begins.

The parameter card contains the market structure as well as other variables that are needed for game play. This card has twenty variables. It contains: (1) the number of teams (up to ten) that are competing; (2) the number of copies of the printed output desired; and (3) eighteen other game parameters. Figures 4.4 and 4.5 illustrate the format and the variables contained on this card. Actually, the instructor can modify the game as he chooses through manipulating the parameter card. A later section of this chapter describes the necessary procedures for parameter card changes and provides explanations of the effects on the environment.

The History Deck. The beginning history deck is composed of sixty-one cards, enough history for ten teams to play. This deck must be placed directly behind the parameter card. The first card contains certain history parameters which relate to next period's play (see Figure 4.6). The next six cards are history for firm one and show the company's product and raw materials beginning inventories, its capacities, debt position, etc. Figures 4.7, 4.8, 4.9, 4.10, 4.11, and 4.12 indicate the variable names and format included in the six history cards for each firm. Each subsequent set of six cards represents, respectively, history for firms two, three, four, . . . , and ten.

If the administrator wishes to use ten firms, the history deck needs no changing. However, if it is desired to utilize less than ten teams--for example, five--two modifications must be made:

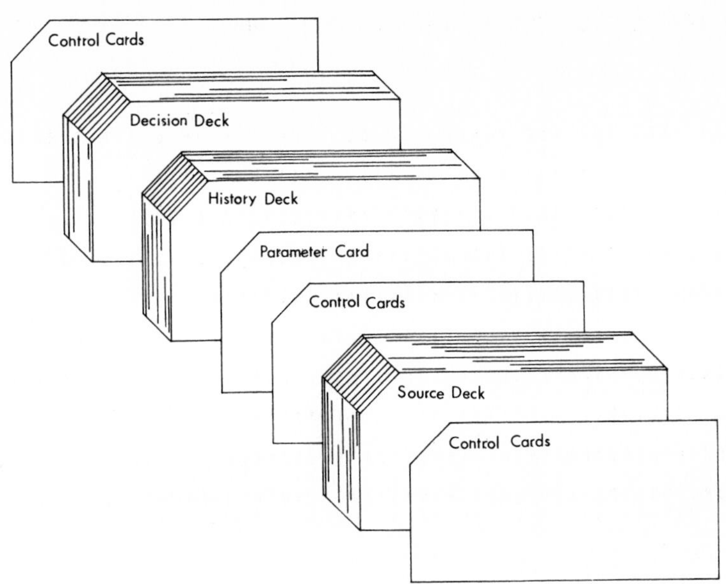

Figure 4-3. Sequential Arrangement of the Source Deck, the Parameter Card, the History Deck, and the Decision Deck with Control Cards Added by the Computer Center.

10 2 75 65 100 50 150 45024 9100100 1000 500 20 2 2 15 20 15 0

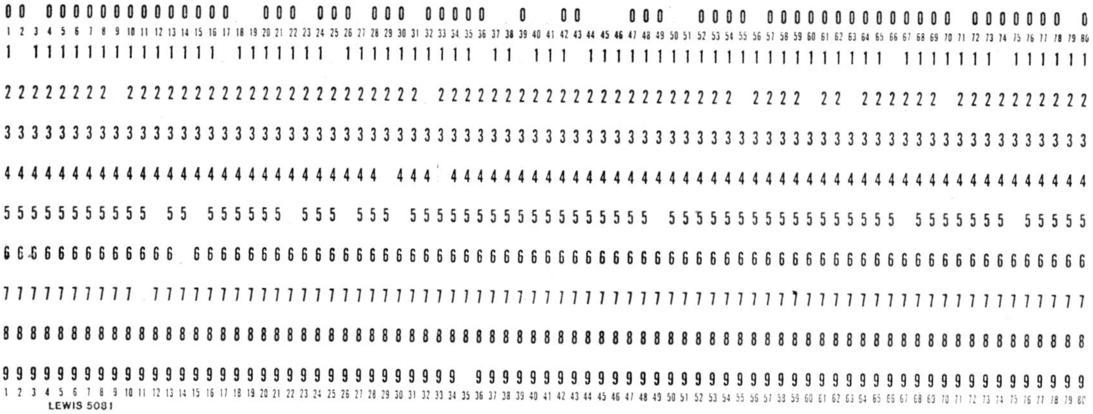

LEWIS 5081

FIELD	VARIABLE CODE	VARIABLE DESCRIPTION
Cols. 1-3	IT	No. of Teams in an Industry.
7-9	IT2	No. of Printouts for Each Team
10-12	PR1	Price of Product One
13-15	PR2	Price of Product Two
16-19	RPR1	Price of Raw Materials 1
20-23	RPR2	Price of Raw Materials 2
24-27	RPR3	Price of Raw Materials 3
28-31	XXL	Industry Wage Rate
32-33	BD	Probability of a Machine Breakdown
34-35	BD1	Probability of Breakdown on Machine 4
36-38	QR1	Fluctuation Index for Demand - Product One
39-41	QR2	Fluctuation Index for Demand - Product Two
42-46	Q1	First Coefficient for Product One Demand
47-51	Q2	First Coefficient for Product Two Demand
52-56	Q11	Second Coefficient for Product One Demand
57-61	Q22	Second Coefficient for Product Two Demand
62-64	UCC1	Unit Carrying Cost for Product One
65-67	UCC2	Unit Carrying Cost for Product Two
68-71	XINT	Interest Rate
72-75	DIV	Earnings Rate on Short-Term Securities
76-80	BEN	Benefits Per Labor Hour

Figure 4.4. The Parameter Card Format for Structuring the OPSIM Environment.

	PARAMETER	FIELD COLUMNS	UNITS	EXAMPLE
1.	Number of Teams	1-3	5	0 0 5
2.	Number of Copies of Printout	8-9	2	0 1
3.	Price of Product One	10-12	80	0 8 0
4.	Price of Product Two	13-15	70	0 7 0
5.	Price of Raw Material 1	16-19	1.00	0 1 0 0
6.	Price of Raw Material 2	20-23	.50	0 0 5 0
7.	Price of Raw Material 3	24-27	1.50	0 1 5 0
8.	Wage Rate	28-31	4.50	0 4 5 0
9.	Probability of Machine Breakdown	32-33	.24	2 4
10.	Probability of Machine 4 Breakdown	34-35	.09	0 9
11.	Product One Fluctuation Index	36-38	1.00	1 0 0
12.	Product Two Fluctuation Index	39-41	1.00	1 0 0
13.	First Coefficient - Product One Demand	42-46	1000.	0 1 0 0 0
14.	First Coefficient - Product Two Demand	47-51	500.	0 0 5 0 0
15.	Second Coefficient for Product One Demand	52-56	20.	0 0 0 2 0
16.	Second Coefficient for Product Two Demand	57-61	20.	0 0 0 2 0
17.	Unit Carrying Cost - Product One	62-64	.20	0 2 0
18.	Unit Carrying Cost - Product Two	65-67	.15	0 1 5
19.	Interest Rate	68-71	.020	0 0 2 0
20.	Earnings Rate on Short-Term Securities	72-75	.015	0 0 1 5
21.	Benefits per Direct Labor Hour	76-80		0 0 0 0 0

Figure 4.5. Parameter Identification and Field Location.

1 45862510.

FIELD	VARIABLE CODE	VARIABLE DESCRIPTION
Cols. 1-3	I	Period Number
4-15	Ran	Random Variable Generated by Sub-Routine

Figure 4.6. Card Format and Variable Names for the First Card in the History Deck.

1 1 17000. 20000. 510000. 610000. 300000. 565520.

LEWIS 5081

FIELD	VARIABLE CODE	VARIABLE DESCRIPTION
Cols. 1-6	-	Used Only for Original History Deck
7-17	BIP1(J)	Beginning Inventory Product One Team (J)
18-28	BIP2(J)	Beginning Inventory Product Two Team (J)
29-40	BRM1(J)	Beginning Inventory Raw Material 1 Team (J)
41-52	BRM2(J)	Beginning Inventory Raw Material 2 Team (J)
53-64	BRM3(J)	Beginning Inventory Raw Material 3 Team (J)
65-76	VBF1(J)	Value Beginning Inventory Finished Goods Product One Team (J)

Figure 4.7. Format and Variable Names for the First History Card for a Given Team.

808000.   510000.   305000.   450000.   2100.   500.

LEWIS 5081

FIELD	VARIABLE CODE	VARIABLE DESCRIPTION
Cols. 1-12	VBF2(J)	Value Beginning Inventory Finished Goods Product Two Team (J)
13-24	VBRI1(J)	Value Beginning Raw Materials 1 Inventory Team (J)
25-36	VBRI2(J)	Value Beginning Raw Materials 2 Inventory Team (J)
37-48	VBRI3(J)	Value Beginning Raw Materials 3 Inventory Team (J)
49-60	C1(J)	Production Capacity Machine 1 in Hours Team (J)
61-72	C2(J)	Production Capacity Machine 2 in Hours Team (J)

Figure 4.8. Format and Variable Names of the Second History Card for a Given Team.

1000.   900.   0.   0.   0.   0.

FIELD	VARIABLE CODE	VARIABLE DESCRIPTION
Cols. 1-12	C3(J)	Production Capacity Machine 3 in Hours Team (J)
13-24	C4(J)	Production Capacity Machine 4 in Hours Team (J)
25-36	CS1(J)	Cumulative Sales of Product One Team (J)
37-48	CS2(J)	Cumulative Sales of Product Two Team (J)
49-60	CCG1(J)	Cumulative Cost of Goods Sold Product One Team (J)
61-72	CCG2(J)	Cumulative Cost of Goods Sold Product Two Team (J)

Figure 4.9. Format and Variable Names of the Third History Card for a Given Team.

0. 0. 0. 160. 640. 100.

FIELD	VARIABLE CODE	VARIABLE DESCRIPTION
Cols. 1-12	CMT(J)	Cumulative Cost of Maintenance Team (J)
13-24	CCOC(J)	Cumulative Carrying and Order Cost for All Raw Materials Team (J)
25-36	CCSC(J)	Cumulative Carrying and Setup Cost for Finished Products Team (J)
37-48	BO1(J)	Back Order Product One From Last Period in Units Team (J)
49-60	BO2(J)	Back Order Product Two From Last Period in Units Team (J)
61-72	SO11(J)	Sales (in Units) Lost Next Period From Stockout of Product One This Period Team (J)

Figure 4.10. Format and Variable Names of the Fourth History Card for a Given Team.

10. 400. 200. 200000. 500000. 1000000.

LEWIS 5081

FIELD	VARIABLE CODE	VARIABLE DESCRIPTION
Cols. 1-12	SO12(J)	Sales (in Units) Lost Period After Next From Stockout This Period - Product One Team (J)
13-24	SO21(J)	Sales (in Units) Lost Next Period From Stockout This Period - Product Two Team (J)
25-36	SO22(J)	Sales (in Units) Lost Period After Next From Stockout This Period - Product Two Team (J)
37-48	CS(J)	Cash Balance Team (J)
49-60	ACR(J)	Accounts Receivable Team (J)
61-72	FXC(J)	Plant and Equipment in Dollars Team (J)

Figure 4.11. Format and Variable Names of the Fifth History Card for a Given Team.

```
0.      935000.     900000.
```

LEWIS 5081

FIELD	VARIABLE CODE	VARIABLE DESCRIPTION
Cols. 1-12	DBT(J)	Debt Balance Team (J)
13-24	AUBF1(J)	Absorption Value Beginning Inventory Finished Goods Product One Team (J)
25-36	AUBF2(J)	Absorption Value Beginning Inventory Finished Goods Product Two Team (J)

Figure 4.12. Format and Variable Names of the Sixth and Last History Card for a Given Team.

1. The first card from the parameter deck should be removed and repunched. The number ten punched, in column 5 and 6, should be changed to correspond to the desired number of teams. If five firms are desired, a five should be punched in column 6. The rest of the card is to be repunched as it is upon receipt from the publisher, leaving column 5 blank.

2. If only five firms are to be used, the history deck should be composed of only the first history card plus six history cards for each team, or only the first 31 cards should be used. Another way of looking at the same idea is that for each of the ten teams not used, six cards should be removed from the bottom of the history deck (in the case of five teams not used, 30 cards should be removed from the bottom of the history deck). Now the history deck is ready to be placed in its proper sequence and run.

The Decision Deck. The initial decision deck is designed for ten firms; therefore, it contains ten cards, one decision card for each firm. Figure 4.13 indicates the format required for entering each variable on the decision card. If the game supervisor wishes to use less than ten teams, for example X teams, the first X decision cards should be used for play and the remaining cards discarded. With this modification, the decision deck is ready to be placed after the history deck.

However, on the next run, a decision card must be prepared by each team using the format shown in Figure 4.13. Upon receiving these new cards, the administrator places the decision cards in order--from firm 1 to firm X. The new decision cards are then placed behind the new history cards, which are last period's punched output.

Running the Program. Now that the card decks have been placed in the correct order to form one complete deck, the administrator should take it to the computer center for advice and help in getting the program to run. A computer center technician can add the appropriate control cards and run the game for the instructor.

The subroutine which generates random numbers for use in the main program follows the source program. Some compilers require that a control card be inserted between the source deck proper and this subroutine. The subroutine deck is not shown in Figure 3.13, since it follows, and is considered part of the source deck.

Diagnostics.

The source program is written in a simplified version of Fortran; therefore, the game should run without difficulty. If trouble is encountered, a printout of the program is given in Appendix B. The computer technician should be shown this printout for diagnostic purposes. Compilers differ slightly between systems and from one computer center to the next, and, therefore, slight changes to the source program may be necessary. More than likely, any differences will be found in the input-output statements and can be easily corrected.

In order to "check out" the OPSIM program, the decision and history decks for period 1 should be run. The source program and the other period 1 decks are obtained by writing either the publisher or the following address:

Dr. Bill R. Darden
Himes Hall, Box 93
College of Business
Louisiana State University
Baton Rouge, Louisiana. 70803

The printout obtained from this test run should match that shown in Chapter III in the section on reporting. If initial printout (consisting of the Managerial Operating Report, the Balance Sheet, the Absorption Operating Statement, the Accounting and Marketing Information Report, and the Industry Report) does not match the exhibits shown in Chapter III, then the following areas should be examined:

1. Does the program printoff match that shown in Appendix B? If the source program printouts do not match, then change the source deck so that it will correspond to that of Appendix B.

2. Does the parameter card have the same parameters in the same columns as shown in Figure 4.4? If not, repunch this card with the correct numbers shown in the manual.

3. Are the history cards in the correct sequence for each team? Are all the card decks in the correct order and are the control cards placed in the correct positions? Remember, the random number subroutine may need to be separated from the source program by a control card.

4. Are the history cards punched correctly? Remember, there are six history cards per team and the history for any team in the initial run should match the history of any other team.

```
1    1  15000  20000  500000  600000  400000 8200 3 0 0 0 0      0      0   0

0000000000    000    000     000     000     000  000 0 0 0 0000000 0000000 0000
1 2 3 4 5 6 7 8 9 10 11 12 13 14 15 16 17 18 19 20 21 22 23 24 25 26 27 28 29 30 31 32 33 34 35 36 37 38 39 40 41 42 43 44 45 46 47 48 49 50 51 52 53 54 55 56 57 58 59 60 61 62 63 64 65 66 67 68 69 70 71 72 73 74 75 76 77 78 79 80
1 111 11 111111111111111111111111111111111111111111111111111111111111111111111111
2222222222222 222222222222222222222222222222222222 222222222222222222222222222222222222
3333333333333333333333333333333333333333333333333 3333333333333333333333333333333
4444444444444444444444444444444444444444444444 4444444444444444444444444444444444
555555555 5555555555555 555555555555555555555555555555555555555555555555555555555
66666666666666666666666666666666666666 6666666666666666666666666666666666666666666
77777777777777777777777777777777777777777777777777777777777777777777777777777777
8888888888888888888888888888888888888888888888888888 8888888888888888888888888888
99999999999999999999999999999999999999999999999999999999999999999999999999999999
1 2 3 4 5 6 7 8 9 10 11 12 13 14 15 16 17 18 19 20 21 22 23 24 25 26 27 28 29 30 31 32 33 34 35 36 37 38 39 40 41 42 43 44 45 46 47 48 49 50 51 52 53 54 55 56 57 58 59 60 61 62 63 64 65 66 67 68 69 70 71 72 73 74 75 76 77 78 79 80
LEWIS 5081
```

FIELD	VARIABLE CODE	VARIABLE DESCRIPTION
Cols. 1-3	J	OPSIM Firm Number
4-6	I	Period of Play
7-13	DP1(J)	Decision Product One Team (J)
14-20	DP2(J)	Decision Product Two Team (J)
21-28	DRM1(J)	Decision Raw Material 1 Team (J)
29-36	DRM2(J)	Decision Raw Material 2 Team (J)
37-44	DRM3(J)	Decision Raw Material 3 Team (J)
45-49	DLH(J)	Decision Direct Labor Hours Team (J)
50-51	DML(J)	Decision Maintenance Workers Team (J)
52-53	XIC1(J)	Investment Capacity Machine 1 Team (J)
54-55	SIC2(J)	Investment Capacity Machine 2 Team (J)
56-57	XIC3(J)	Investment Capacity Machine 3 Team (J)
58-59	SCI4(J)	Investment Capacity Machine 4 Team (J)
60-67	PYMT(J)	Payment of Debt Team (J)
68-75	DSEC(J)	Decision Short-Term Securities Team (J)
76-80	PEN(J)	Penalties Assessed Against Team (J) by the Administrator

Figure 4.13. Formats and Variable Names for Decision Card for A Given Team in a Given Period of Play.

5. Are the decision cards punched correctly? Again, each firm should have the same set of initial decisions.

6. The output of Firm One alone for the initial run should match the output printout shown in Chapter III. The random element in OPSIM will cause other firms' printouts to be slightly dissimilar, but only within narrow ranges.

If the computer center personnel cannot run the OPSIM source program, Appendices A, B, C, and D should be consulted. Appendix A contains an alphabetical listing of all program variables. Appendix B is a printout of the Fortran II source program. Cross-referencing Appendix A with Appendix B will allow the technician to follow the program logic. Appendix C is a flow diagram and provides a visual look at how the program is controlled.

Appendix D provides help in adjusting the OPSIM program to various kinds of computer systems. For certain systems, program segmentation is necessary and advice is given on how and where to segment the Fortran source program.

Description of OPSIM Card Formats.

The instructor using OPSIM is not required to perform any computations nor to prepare any reports in the course of the game. The administration of OPSIM is limited to the preparation of input cards for the current period decisions and, also, the substitution of the newly punched history cards for the currently used history deck.

Decision Card Formats. Figure 4.13 shows both the variables and variable format for a typical decision card. The fields of the different decisions are identified in the text below the card. For reference to the OPSIM computer program, the code descriptions are also shown in Figure 4.13. The student must make decisions in terms of the unit of account for each particular decision area. For example, direct labor must be ordered in terms of hours, not in terms of dollars. Investments must be made in terms of the number of machines desired.

The last field (columns 76-80) is available for the instructor to penalize any specific team. Typical penalties might include: (1) assessment for late decisions - $50,000; (2) incompetent behavior in the form of "jester decisions" - $40,000; (3) demonstration of lack of preparation or research in decision making - $75,000; and (4) technical errors such as incorrect punching of the decision cards - $25,000.

All decisions for a given firm are entered on one decision card. The respective card fields are oriented in the usual right to left numerical sequence (right adjusted fields). Since decimals are not used, the unit column is the extreme right, while the tens column is the second column from the right margin of a given field, etc. Therefore, a decision for 100 units would be punched in the last three columns to the right with the "1" being punched in the third column from the right margin of the respective field. The fields for the various decision areas are illustrated in Figure 4-14. In preparing the decision cards, it is not necessary to punch zeroes to the left of the decision numbers to complete the field. Thus, in a six-column field, "000100" could be punched, or the card would show "   100" in the field, leaving blank the first three columns.

Special attention should be given to decision provided for Management to invest in short-term securities. Investment can be made in any dollar amount up to $999,999,999 in columns 68 to 75. Since investment in short-term securities can take place at any time, "disinvestment" can also take place at any time--<u>in the same field</u> (<u>columns 68 to 75</u>). However, <u>"disinvestment" must be preceded by a minus (-) sign</u> in column 68 which means that "disinvestment" is restricted to $9,999,999.

<u>History Card Formats</u>. All of the data from past periods for each firm relevant to future operations are stored in history cards. Figures 4-6 through 4-12 illustrate the data that are held in external memory in the form of cards. The exhibits also show the field location and field widths of the data. After the processing of the decisions of a given period, the computer updates the history cards and then produces a new deck of history cards that must be used for the next period's decisions. All teams start with identical history data but after the processing of the first decisions, each team's history cards are different, <u>i.e.</u>, unless they, by chance, make identical decisions. Therefore, it is imperative that the new history cards be used for processing the next period's decisions.

<u>How to Change the Game Structure: The "Fingertip" Control Card</u>

The game structure provided in OPSIM with the original parameter card, can provide experience in decision-making for the students over many periods of play; however, through changing the parameter card the instructor can provide dynamic cases to reinforce the techniques taught in the classroom.

Figure 4-14 reproduces the parameter card shown in Figure 4-4. Moving from left to right along the card in Figure 4-14, a description follows for each parameter:

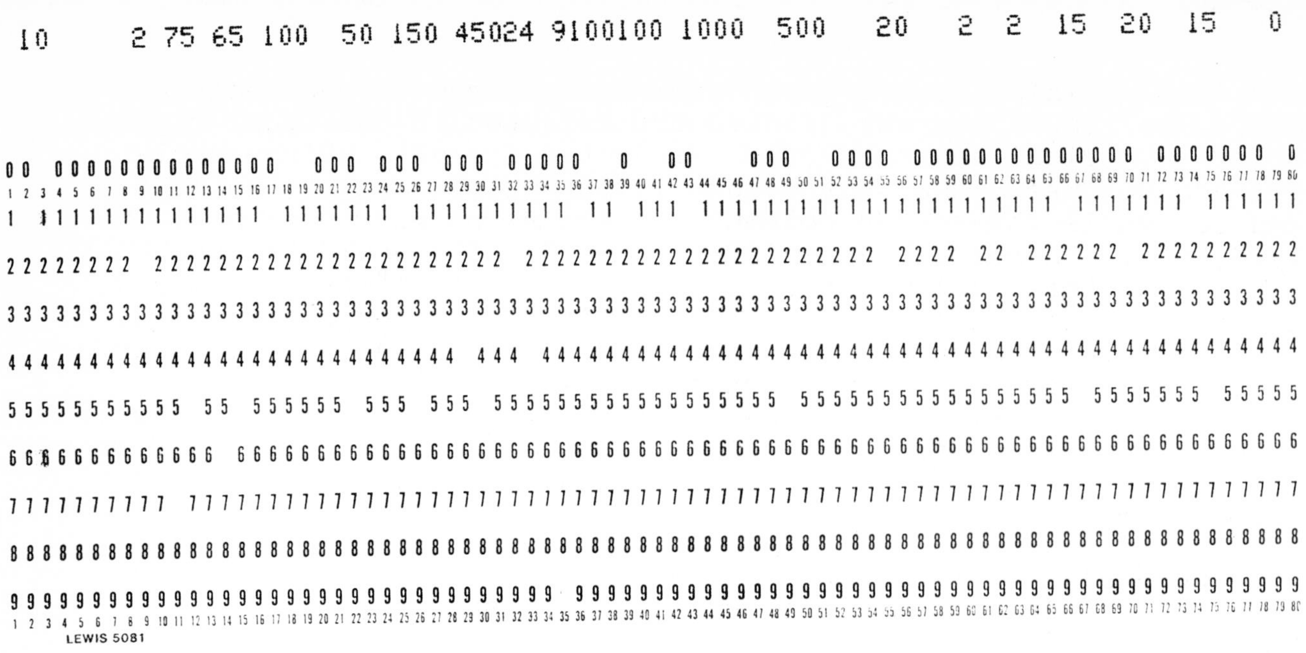

10 2 75 65 100 50 150 45024 9100100 1000 500 20 2 2 15 20 15 0

LEWIS 5081

FIELD	VARIABLE CODE	VARIABLE DESCRIPTION
Cols. 1-3	IT	No. of Team in an Industry.
7-9	IT2	No. of Printouts for Each Team.
10-12	PR1	Price of Product One.
13-15	PR2	Price of Product Two.
16-19	RPR1	Price of Raw Materials 1.
20-23	RPR2	Price of Raw Materials 2.
24-27	RPR3	Price of Raw Materials 3.
28-31	XXL	Industry Wage Rate.
32-33	BD	Probability of a Machine Breakdown.
34-35	BD1	Probability of Breakdown on Machine 4.
36-38	QR1	Fluctuation Index for Demand - Product One.
39-41	QR2	Fluctuation Index for Demand - Product Two.
42-46	Q1	First Coefficient for Product One Demand.
47-51	Q2	First Coefficient for Product Two Demand.
52-56	Q11	Second Coefficient for Product One Demand.
57-61	Q22	Second Coefficient for Product Two Demand.
62-64	UCC1	Unit Carrying Cost for Product One.
65-67	UCC2	Unit Carrying Cost for Product Two.
68-71	XINT	Interest Rate.
72-75	DIV	Earnings Rate on Short-Term Securities.
76-80	BEN	Benefits per Labor Hour

Figure 4.14. The Parameter Card Format for Structuring the OPSIM Environment.

1. The first constant indicates the number of firms that are competing. It is punched in columns 1, 2, and 3. The initial parameter card calls for ten teams; therefore, a "one" is punched in column 2 and a "zero" is punched in column 3, <u>right adjusted</u> as shown below. The maximum number of teams that can be used is ten;

Cols. 1-3 No. of Firms	0	1	0
	Col. 1	Col. 2	Col. 3

Field Width

however, by repunching column 2 and column 3, less than ten teams can be used. For example, if five firms are desired for game play, the team number field should be repunched as below.

Cols. 1-3 No. of Firms	0	0	5
	Col. 1	Col. 2	Col. 3

It should be recalled that modifications must also be made to the history deck when using less than ten teams.

2. Columns 8 and 9 are used to indicate the number of copies of each printout desired. In Figure 4-14 the instructor can see that two copies of each report will be printed. If ten copies are needed, the changes in columns 8 and 9 are shown below.

Cols. 8-9 No. of Printouts	1	0
	Col. 8	Col. 9

3. Finished Goods market prices can be manipulated to either "tighten up the game" or to "loosen up the game". Therefore, while the student cannot affect prices (since OPSIM is an internally oriented game), the instructor can change prices at will. However, it is recommended that announcements be made to the class several playing periods before each price change.

Columns 10, 11 and 12 are used for recording the price of Product One, while columns 13, 14 and 15 define the field for the price of Product Two. On the initial parameter card the prices are $75 and $65 respectively for Product One and Product Two. Figure 4-14 indicates a "zero" in column 10, a "seven" in column 11 and a "five" in column 12, indicating the price for Product One. Also, there is a "zero" in column 13, a "six" in column 14 and a "five" in column

15, indicating a price of $65 for Product Two.

Cols. 10-12 Price-Product One	1	0	0
	Col. 10	Col. 11	Col. 12

Cols. 13-15 Price-Product Two	0	9	0
	Col. 13	Col. 14	Col. 15

The correct punches for changing product prices to $100 and $90 for Products One and Two, respectively, are shown above.

4. Raw Material prices can also be changed at will by the instructor. Briefly, the prices provided on the initial parameter card are $1.00, $ .50 and $1.50 for Raw Materials One, Two and Three The formats for these prices are shown below.

Cols. 16-19 Price - Raw Materials One	0	1	0	0
	Col. 16	Col. 17	Col. 18	Col. 19

Cols. 20-23 Price - Raw Materials Two	0	0	5	0
	Col. 20	Col. 21	Col. 22	Col. 23

Cols. 24-27 Price - Raw Materials Three	0	1	5	0
	Col. 24	Col. 25	Col. 26	Col. 27

Notice that the prices need no decimal, but digits for two decimal places are always included. Further, the digits are "right adjusted' that is, the last digit is always placed in the rightmost column in the field.

5. Direct Labor wage rate can be increased or decreased to any level desired. Appearing in columns 28 through 31, wages are initially $4.50 and appear as "450", rather than $4.50" (see Figures 4-5 and 4-14).

Cols. 28-31 Wage Parameter	0	4	9	0
	Col. 28	Col. 29	Col. 30	Col. 31

An example of a wage change by the instructor is shown above. Wages are now $4.90 per hour.

6. To change the probability of a machine breakdown, the digits in columns 32 and 33 must be changed. The parameter card now has a "two" in column 32 and a "four" punched in column 33, indicating that the probability of a breakdown is approximately .24.

Columns 32-33 Probability of a Machine Breakdown	5	0
	Col. 32	Col. 33

Above, the correct punches are demonstrated for increasing the probability of machine breakdown to "approximately" .50.

7. Columns 34 and 35 are used to determine the probability of the breakdown of <u>Machine 4</u>. While the two preceding columns determined the <u>total probability</u> of the breakdown of <u>all</u> machines, this additional field indicates only the probability of Machine 4 breaking down. Thus, the probability of a machine other than Machine 4 breaking down is the total breakdown probability minus the probability of Machine 4 breaking down. In the initial parameter deck, the breakdown probability of Machine 4 is .09; therefore, the probability of some other machine breaking down is .24 less .09, or .15. Care should be taken so that the probability of a Machine 4 breakdown is not greater than the probability for all machine breakdowns. The correct punches for changing the breakdown probability of Machine 4 from .09 to .15 is given below.

Cols. 34-35 Breakdown Probability of Machine 4	1	5
	Col. 34	Col. 35

8. Demand is a function of the period number. However, there are internally generated random fluctuations around the trend by increasing or decreasing the digits in columns 36, 37 and 38 for Product One and the digits in columns 39, 40 and 41 for Product Two. For example, a "two" punched in column 36 and "zeros" punched in columns 37 and 38 doubles the range of random movements around the demand trend for Product One. Figure 4-15 shows a proposed relationship between trend demand for Product One and the time period. The solid line shows trend demand, while the two dotted lines indicate the range of demand possibilities. In period two, the range of possible fluctuations around Product One demand trend is increased 153% as shown below.

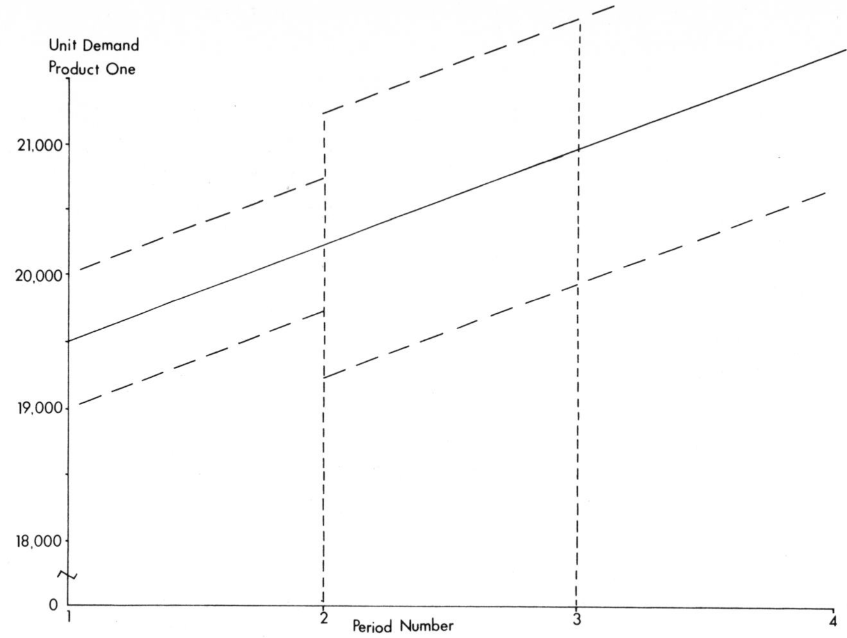

Figure 4-15. Demonstration of the Effect of Doubling the Range of Possible Fluctuations Around the Demand Trend.

Cols. 36-38 Dispersion Index Product One	2	5	3
	Col. 36	Col. 37	Col. 38

The random fluctuations around the trend demand for Product Two can be influenced in a similar manner in the field provided by columns 39, 40 and 41.

9. The instructor also has at his disposal the ability to change the slopes of product trend demand. Both Products One and Two each have two coefficient, reflecting second degree polynomials. Initially, the second coefficient for each product have values of zero; therefore, each product's demand trend is a straight line (see Figure 4-16 for Product One).

In many cases the instructor may wish to increase or decrease the slope of product demand trend. Figure 4-16 shows that for periods 1 and 2 trend demand increases by one thousand units each period. However, in period 3, the trend demand has been increased by 1500 units. To accomplish this task, columns 42, 43, 44, 45 and 46 on the parameter card must be repunched from "1000" to "1500". (See below). The first coefficient of Product Two is contained in columns

Cols. 42-46 First Coefficient of Product One	0	1	5	0	0
	Col. 42	Col. 43	Col. 44	Col. 45	Col. 46

47, 48, 49, 50 and 51 of the parameter card. In addition, columns 52, 53, 54, 55 and 56 and columns 57, 58, 59, 60 and 61 define the fields of the second coefficients of trend demand for Product One and Product Two, respectively. Values entered into these columns change the trend demand equations into second degree polynomials. (See Figure 4-17.) Thus, the instructor has complete freedom to change the structure of product demands to continue the learning experiences of the student in Operations Management.

10. Carrying charges per unit of average finished goods inventories can be manipulated. Rationales for such changes include increases in insurance premiums, changes in warehousing charges, etc. The relationship between raw materials and finished goods form the basis for many Operations Management strategies. The parameter card contains the unit carrying charge for Product One in columns 62, 63 and 64. The unit carrying charge for Product Two is shown in columns 65, 66 and 67 and initially this charge is \$ .15 per unit. The format below shows how the charge for Product Two can be increased to \$ .25 per unit average inventory.

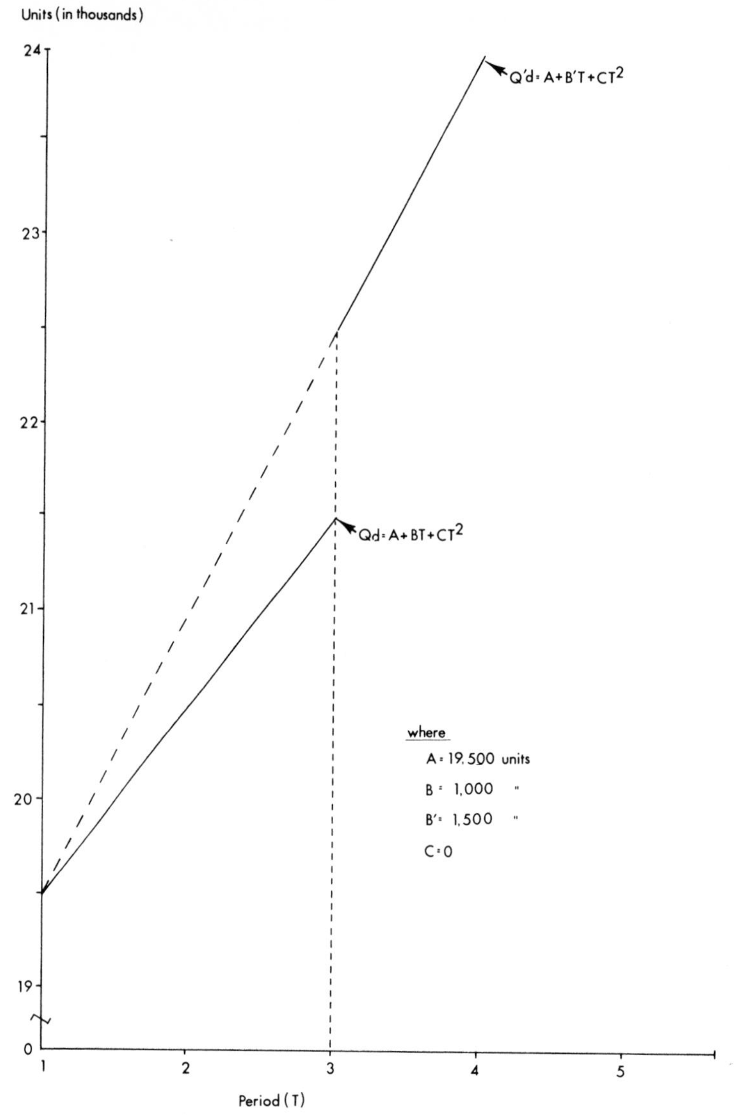

Figure 4-16. Changes in Product One's Demand Trend Slope.

Cols. 65-67
Carrying Charge Per
Unit of Product Two

0	2	5
Col. 65	Col. 66	Col. 67

11. The interest rate on debt and the earnings rate on short-term securities can be changed to reflect changing money market conditions. The interest rate is contained on the parameter card in columns 68, 69, 70 and 71 (see Figure 4-14). The earnings rate for short-term securities is contained in columns 72, 73, 74 and 75. Since OPSIM management can invest excess cash reserves in these securities, shifting the earnings rate--with appropriate warnings--can help the student in gaining insights into investment alternatives. A change in the short-term earnings rate (based strictly on cost) from 1.5% to 1.1% is demonstrated below.

Cols. 72-75
Short-term
Earnings Rate

0	0	1	1
Col. 72	Col. 73	Col. 74	Col. 75

12. In addition to wages, direct labor can receive benefits if the instructor so desires. Benefits are paid on a per direct labor hour basis and unit benefits are punched on the parameter card in columns 76 through 79. This parameter is initially assigned a value of zero; however, a demonstration of how the parameter may be repunched to $ .50 is shown below.

Cols. 76-79
Benefits per
Direct Labor Hour

0	0	5	0
76	77	78	79

Model II of the Decision Making Game

An advanced version of OPSIM is available which incorporates the basic OPSIM I into an interactive business game. In OPSIM II the participating firms are allowed to make price decisions--as well as the other decisions already in OPSIM I--and the pricing policy of each firm affects the sales of every other team.

OPSIM II is recommended only for senior and graduate courses--including M.B.A. classes. OPSIM I provides a great deal of realism in Operations Management for most undergraduate courses; particularly since it is designed for teaching students techniques in Operations Research.

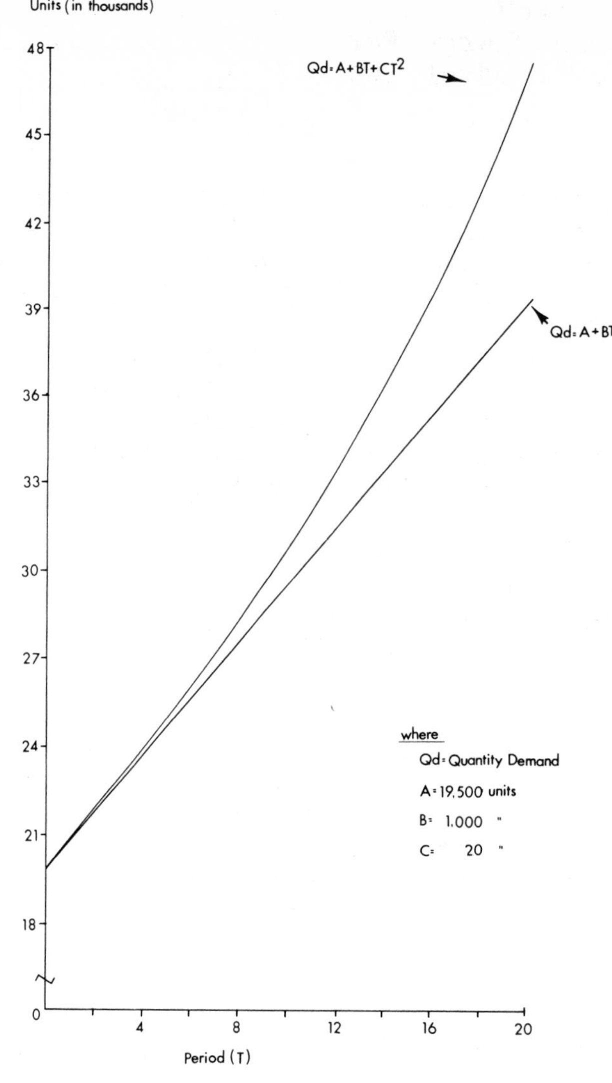

Figure 4-17. The Effect of a Second Coefficient Change from "0" to "20" on the Demand Trend of Product One.

Appendix F provides the additional information needed for the Operation of OPSIM II. The OPSIM II source deck, the initial decision deck, the parameter card and the history deck (all that is needed for the teams to compete) may be obtained from the same source as OPSIM I. Some administrators may wish to start with OPSIM I and then convert to OPSIM II when the students have been properly acclimated to computer games.

Summary

The "fingertip control" parameter card allows the instructor to change the environment of OPSIM in order to teach specific lessons--or to extend the learning experience of production, systems, and accounting students. However, the initial parameter card, unaltered, provides a well-structured production environment within which the student can learn to make operating decisions. If the instructor so desires, he can completely disregard this section on "fingertip parameter control". He can continue to use the initial parameter card for all game plays without greatly affecting the learning experiences made available to his students through OPSIM.

Coordination of Coursework with OPSIM

OPSIM can be used in a multitude of ways to increase the learning experience of students--both in and outside the classroom. This section outlines some of the methods that have been successfully implemented by the authors.

Number and Rate of Game Plays. One of the basic problems facing instructors is the number and rate of game plays. The solution to this problem is determined by such factors as course level, student sophistication, and number of class meetings per week. Below are listed some of the situations and classroom routines found useful:

1. OPSIM is most useful to teachers of operations management. Assuming three one-hour lectures per week (for example, lectures on Monday, Wednesday and Friday), decision cards can be required on the day of the second lecture and the printed output can be returned to the students on the last lecture day. In conjuncture with this plan, the half hour of the last lecture in the week can be given to the class for examining decision output and organizing for making the next set of decisions.

2. If the game structure is not changed, for the average class the learning experience continues through ten to fifteen

plays. However, the instructor will find student learning can be prolonged for an indefinite period through ingenious changes of the parameter card; therefore, changing the production environment provides new lessons.

How to Organize into OPSIM Firms. OPSIM firms can be organized on a functional basis, or team functional assignments need not be made. In either case, it is most helpful to have firm "captains" These "captains" are responsible for arranging firm meetings, production analysis assignments, and organizing for class presentations Actually, most classes agree that organizing along functional lines-with the responsibility for specific areas assigned to specific individuals--has little benefit and is probably inefficient. These classes have found that the pooling of information over all areas and the making of joint decisions provides much greater insight into the long-run and short-run nature of operations management.

The Use of Board Meetings. In connection with OPSIM play, board meetings can be called for each team after a number of plays. These meetings serve the purpose of providing checkpoints so that the efficiency and the extent of participation by the various members of the teams can be examined.

At the board meetings, students should be required--through graphs, projections and oral presentations--to present prior strategies with results and future plans, with projections justifying the use of these strategies. Explanations of all phases of prior decisions, with evaluation of errors, provides a learning experience that is unique.

To enhance the importance of board meetings and to bring additional experience to bear on the problems faced by the students in the OPSIM environment, a faculty member can be appointed to each board. The faculty member serves as the focal point for all oral presentations and should question all phases of managerial strategy.

Role Playing. Most batch process computer business simulations do not provide for the human side of the firm. At the outset, provisions are made for functional relationships between dollar quantities invested in training programs and sales, between investments in employee benefits and productivity, etc. However, with the use of the "fingertip control" parameter card, a golden opportunity is available to set up "collective bargaining sessions."

In order to prepare for collective bargaining sessions, the instructor announces the following rules:

1. Each firm has a contract with its respective union that determines the dollar wage. From experience, excellent results

are obtained from five period contracts.

2. Assuming industry-wide bargaining units, each team selects a member to represent them on the management bargaining team. Another alternative is to have bargaining sessions for individual firms. While the latter approach involves more work for the instructor, either method yields excellent results.

3. Prior to the session, the instructor sets some minumum wage and/or labor benefits, below which the union will strike. This minimum package is not known to the student industry bargaining unit.

4. The instructor either represents the union or selects some knowledgable person or persons to serve in this capacity. The union bargaining unit is armed with industry profit figures, demand trends, information on how other industries fare and other argumentative information.

5. Bargaining now takes place between the units, without the management unit knowing the minimum "strike" package and the labor unit trying to push wages as high as possible.

6. If, after one hour, no agreement is reached or the management team still insists upon a wage lower than the minimum acceptable wage, then a "strike" is declared. If, however, some agreement is reached, then the instructor adjusts the wage parameter on the "finger-tip control" card to the agreed upon wage.

7. If a strike is declared, the program is still run for the next period; however, a "strike" card is inserted between statements number 46 and 47. The "strike" card has the following format:

Col. No.	D	L	H	(	J	)	=	0	.
	7	8	9	10	11	12	13	14	15

After receiving the output from the above run, another bargaining session is held. This procedure is repeated until a "steelement" is reached. At this time another contract is in effect for five more periods, at which time another bargaining session will commence.

It is important that the instructor provide a "minimum acceptable wage" for effective bargaining sessions. This wage should be so chosen to teach particular object lessions which are reflective of real world bargaining problems. A versatile instructor will recognize that wages and/or other parameters available on the "finger-tip control" card can be adjusted upward or downward to reflect increases in employee benefits. In summary, OPSIM can be a potent pedigogical tool when combined with "role playing".

CHAPTER V

OPERATIONS RESEARCH AND DECISION MAKING

Increasingly, management is seeking better and more reliable methods of making decisions. Much business research is directed toward finding operational relationships which provide bases for management policy. Since World II, a body of knowledge and methods has been accumulated which management has found useful for decision making: this core of techniques has been termed "Operations Research."

Operations Research has its origin in World War II where it was employed to solve specific problems calling for multiple skills from many disciplines. Thus, initially, Operations Research involved a "team" or "Task Force" approach to problem solving and brought to bear, simultaneously, the skills of experts needed to produce the desired results. Over time, a successful core of knowledge has emerged which is now thought of as being operations research.

The advancing levels of hardware and software computer technology has proven to be the catalyst that has caused business managers to consider the use of Operations Research within their own firms. Traditionally, the complexity of the operations of modern business has discouraged the use of scientific methods of analysis. Managers developed "rules of thumb" to provide guides for better decisions. The advent of modern computer technology has opened new frontiers to theorists and practitioners of business management--especially the internal area of Operations Management. Here are some of the effects of computer technology:

1. For the first time, total information systems appear feasible (total information systems are actually installed and operational in some firms).

2. The "systems philosophy" of business management is a distinct possibility for any size firm. The integrative powers of the computer, its potential for management control, and its information storage and retrieval powers offer characteristics which substantially decrease "suboptimization," even in the largest of firms.

3. Many decision making techniques (or algorithms) can now be successfully implemented by business management. The computer can quickly carry out the grueling, time-consuming and boring computations that successive iterations of such proce-

dures typically require to arrive at optimum solutions.

Management theorists point out that success in utilizing Operations Research depends upon the degree of "structure" of the problems to which it may be applied. Herbert A. Simon indicates that well-structured problems are particularly amenable to the techniques of Operations Research (see: Simon, The Shape of Automation, Harper and Row, 1965). Well-structured problems are easily modeled, since their variables are known, measurable and easily interrelated.

The degree of problem "structureness" is believed to be related to the level within the organization at which the decision is made. Decisions at the higher levels of organization are considered ill-structured and require subjective decision making routines on the part of management. The lower levels of management, however, are considered well-structured, and this is the sphere of management at which Operations Research has been most successfully applied.

Training simulations of the internal operations of the industrial firm provide economical "experience" for management personnel in the use of Operations Research. For example, The Decision Making Game can be used to teach linear programming, EOQ model development, present value analysis--all of which should be in the repertoire of skills possessed by the modern manager.

With the development of computers having higher speeds and greater storage (for example, the IBM Systems 360 - 65, - 75, and - 95 series) the actual simulation of the entire firm becomes a distinct possibility. Some pioneer work involving a paint factory has already demonstrated the feasibility and advantages of such simulations (see: Holt, Modigliani, Muth, and Simon, Planning, Production, Inventories, and Work Force, Prentice-Hall, 1960). It is not too difficult to foresee a time in the future where complex firm-to-industry simulations will be used to evaluate various intermediate strategies of the firm, much as simulation is being used today within the firm to determine decision rules.

Closer government regulation and the implicit cooperativeness that is observed between large firms in increasing returns to scale industries leads one to believe that the environment for simulation is becoming more and more well-structured. Econometric analyses are providing more information to the firm about its interactions with industry, society and the national economy --providing bases and requirements for more optimal predictions and planning. The pioneering work of Jay Forrester (see, for example: J. W. Forrester, Industrial Dynamics, Wiley, New York, 1961) has demonstrated to management the advantages of simulating the "flows" of materials, men, money, and products throughout the firm's total system.

Executive training programs are beginning to turn to simulations to teach Operations Research and to provide an integrated view of intrafirm functions. Fritz A. McCameron at Louisiana State University reports excellent training results from the use of business games as a capstone exercise on the Mid-South Executive Development Program. Experimentation is now in progress to provide executives with Operations Research computer routines for decision purposes while playing executive games. This feature teaches executives <u>to recognize</u> problems for which specific Operations Research techniques are applicable--even where the executive does not know the mechanics of a particular quantitative approach.

In summary, Operations Research is providing a growing body of advanced techniques to aid executives in decision making. However, such a body of knowledge is not of use to business executives if they are not trained in its use. Several reasons explain why executives do not use Operations Research: first, they are afraid to apply O.R. because of the uncertain economic outcomes; second, they prefer not to apply what they do not understand; third, they are not trained in the use of O.R. techniques; and fourth, they do not recognize the problems that O.R. can solve. The use of OPSIM can solve many of these obstacles to the implementation of O.R. <u>The Decision Making Game</u> and other management games provide a training environment in which executives can practice O.R. and in which costly mistakes do not represent economic ruin to the firm. Decision simulations, such as OPSIM, also provide a <u>hidden</u> characteristic; managers intuitively become aware of the problems in which Operations Research techniques can make a substantial contribution.

Every executive should analyze the level of competence in quantitative methods required to carry out the functions of his position effectively and to help him in obtaining promotions. Such an analysis must be made in terms of the management philosophy of the firm (participative management and management by results philosophies indicate wider latitude to use O.R. techniques), the degree to which the firm wishes to employ scientific approaches to achieve efficiency in goal attainment (a scientifically oriented firm would encourage use of the computer in decision making and allow latitude for some experimentation in new methods), and the type of position held (for example, many staff positions require a high mathematical sophistication, while most line executive positions require only enough competence to recognize problems and to communicate with subordinates). Curtiss Jones of the Harvard Business School provides an excellent format for the executive to analyze the O.R. level of competence needed in his position (see: Curtiss Jones, "Applied Mathematics for Businessmen," <u>The Harvard Business Review</u>, 1967).

In the opinion of the authors, here are the best books available for increasing the level of competence in quantitative methods for business (to be used after the executive has determined the necessary level of competence):

I. Sources for executives seeking a beginning to intermediate understanding and require some non-mathematical explanations:

1. Richard I. Levin and C. A. Kirkpatrick. _Quantitative Approaches to Management_. McGraw-Hill, New York, 1966.

2. W. W. Thompson. _Operations Research Techniques_. Merrill, 1967.

3. Harold Bierman, L. Fouraker, and R. K. Jaedike. _Quantitative Analysis for Business Decisions_. Irwin, Homewood, Illinois, 1961.

4. Leonard W. Hein. _The Quantitative Approach to Managerial Decisions_. Prentice-Hall, Englewood Cliffs, New Jersey, 1967.

5. Fritz McCameron. _COBOL: Logic and Programming_. Irwin, Homewood, Illinois, 1966.

6. Richard I. Levin and C. A. Kirkpatrick. _Planning and Control with PERT/CPM_. McGraw-Hill, New York, 1967.

II. Other sources:

1. Billy Goetz. _Quantitative Methods_. McGraw-Hill, 1966.

2. Robert Schaifer. _Probability and Statistics for Business Decisions_. McGraw-Hill, 1959.

3. Robert A. Olsen. _Manufacturing Management: A Quantitative Approach_. International Textbook Company, Scranton, Pennsylvania, 1968.

4. J. W. Forrester. _Industrial Dynamics_. Wiley; New York, 1961.

5. E. H. Bowman and R. B. Fetter, _Analysis for Production Management_. 2d ed. Irwin, Homewood, Illinois, 1961.

6. R. W. Metzger. _Elementary Mathematical Programming_. Wiley, New York, 1963.

7. Robert W. Miller. _Schedule, Cost and Profit Control with PERT_. McGraw-Hill, New York, 1963.

8. C. W. Churchman, R. L. Ackoff, and E. L. Arnoff. Introduction to Operations Research. Wiley, New York, 1957.

9. Kenneth E. Boulding. "General Systems Theory--the Skeleton of Science," Management Science, April, 1956, pp. 197-208.

10. L. Von Bertalenffy. "General Systems Theory: A New Approach to Unity of Science," Human Biology, December, 1951, Vol. 23, pp. 302-361.

11. John Pfeiffer. New Look at Education. Odyssey Press, New Road Poughkeepsie, N. Y., 1968.

12. Charles C. Holt, F. Modigliani, J. F. Muth, and Herbert A. Simon. Planning Production Inventories and Work Force. Prentice-Hall, Englewood Cliffs, N. J., 1960.

13. B. R. Darden. "An Operational Approach to Product Pricing," Journal of Marketing, April, 1968, pp. 29-34.

APPENDICES

APPENDIX A

Definitions of Program Variables for *The Decision Game*

VARIABLE NAME	VARIABLE DEFINITION
ABR1 (J)	Average value of beginning inventory, raw material 1, Team J.
ABR2 (J)	Average value of beginning inventory, raw material 2, Team J.
ABR3 (J)	Average value of beginning inventory, raw material 3, Team J.
ACDP (J)	Absorption cost of current production, Team J.
ACDP1(J)	Absorption cost of current production, Product One, Team J.
ACDP2(J)	Absorption cost of current production, Product Two, Team J.
ACG (J)	Absorption cost of goods sold, Team J.
ACG1 (J)	Absorption cost of goods sold, Product One, Team (J).
ACG2 (J)	Absorption cost of goods sold, Product Two, Team (J).
ACGAS(J)	Absorption cost of goods available for sale, Team (J).
ACGAS1 (J)	Absorption cost of goods available for sale, Product One, Team J.
ACGAS2 (J)	Absorption cost of goods available for sale, Product Two, Team J.
ADMIN (J)	Period Manufacturing overhead, Team J.
ADMIN1(J)	Allocated period manufacturing overhead, Product One, Team J.
ADMIN2(J)	Allocated period manufacturing overhead, Product Two, Team J.
AIRM1 (J)	Average inventory, raw materials 1, Team J.
AIRM2 (J)	Average inventory, raw materials 2, Team J.
AIRM3 (J)	Average inventory, raw materials 3, Team J.
APROM (J)	Absorption production contribution, Team J.
APROM1(J)	Absorption production contribution, Product One, Team J.
APROM2(J)	Absorption production contribution, Product Two, Team J.
AVBF (J)	Absorption value of beginning inventories, Team J.
AVBF1 (J)	Absorption value of beginning inventory, Product One, Team J.
AVBF2 (J)	Absorption value of beginning inventory, Product Two, Team J.

VARIABLE NAME	VARIABLE DEFINITION
BD	Probability of a machine breakdown, any team.
BD1	Probability of a machine 2 breakdown, any team.
BEN	Labor benefits paid per unit of either product produced.
BIP1 (J)	Beginning inventory, Product One, Team J.
BIP2 (J)	Beginning inventory, Product Two, Team J.
BO1 (J)	Backorder, Product One, Team J.
BO2 (J)	Backorder, Product Two, Team J.
BRM1 (J)	Beginning inventory, raw material 1, Team J.
BRM2 (J)	Beginning inventory, raw material 2, Team J.
BRM3 (J)	Beginning inventory, raw material 3, Team J.
C1 (J)	Production capacity of machine 1 in hours, Team J.
C2 (J)	Production capacity of machine 2 in hours, Team J.
C3 (J)	Production capacity of machine 3 in hours, Team J.
C4 (J)	Production capacity of machine 4 in hours, Team J.
CC1	Amount of capacity 1 needed to produce Product Two.
CC3	Amount of capacity 3 needed to produce Product Two.
CC4	Amount of capacity 4 needed to produce Product Two.
CCG1 (J)	Cumulative cost of goods sold of Product One, Team J.
CCG2 (J)	Cumulative cost of goods sold of Product Two, Team J.
CCOC (J)	Cumulative total carrying and order cost of all raw materials, Team J.
CCP (J)	Finished goods carrying cost, Team J.
CCP1 (J)	Carrying cost of Product One, Team J.
CCP2 (J)	Carrying cost of Product Two, Team J.
CCRM (J)	Total carrying cost of raw materials, Team J.
CCRM1(J)	Carrying cost of raw material 1, Team J.
CCRM2(J)	Carrying cost of raw material 2, Team J.
CCRM3(J)	Carrying cost of raw material 3, Team J.
CCSC (J)	Cumulative carrying and setup cost for finished product, Team J.
CDP	Direct cost decision, Products One and Two.
CDP1 (J)	Direct cost decision, Product One, Team J.
CDP2 (J)	Direct cost decision, Product Two, Team J.
CG (J)	Total cost of goods sold, Team J.
CG1 (J)	Cost of goods sold, Product One, Team J.
CG2 (J)	Cost of goods sold, Product Two, Team J.
CGAS (J)	Total cost of goods available for sale, Team J.
CGAS1(J)	Cost of goods available for sale, Product One, Team J.
CGAS2(J)	Cost of goods available for sale, Product Two, Team J.
CLH (J)	Total cost of labor used in production, Team J.
CLH1 (J)	Cost of labor, Product One, Team J.
CLH2 (J)	Cost of labor, Product Two, Team J.
CML (J)	Cost of maintenance labor ($500/worker), Team J.
CMT (J)	Cumulative cost of maintenance, Team J.
COC (J)	Total carrying and order costs for all raw materials, Team J.

VARIABLE NAME	VARIABLE DEFINITION
CONOP(J)	Contribution from operations, Team J.
CRM (J)	Direct cost of raw materials used in production, Team J.
CRM1 (J)	Direct cost, raw material 1, Team J.
CRM2 (J)	Direct cost, raw material 2, Team J.
CRM3 (J)	Direct cost, raw material 3, Team J.
CRM31(J)	Direct cost, raw material 3, for producing Product One, Team J.
CRM32(J)	Direct cost, raw material 3, for producing Product Two, Team J.
CS (J)	Cash account, Team J.
CS1 (J)	Cumulative sales of Product One, Team J.
CS2 (J)	Cumulative sales of Product Two, Team J.
DBT (J)	Amount of debt, Team J.
DEP (J)	Current depreciation, plant and equipment, Team J.
DIV (J)	Earnings rate on short-term securities, Team J.
DLH (J)	Scheduled labor hours, Team J.
DML (J)	Decision number of maintenance workers, Team J.
DP1 (J)	Decision quantity of Product One, Team J.
DP2 (J)	Decision quantity of Product Two, Team J.
DRM1 (J)	Decision quantity of raw material 1, Team J.
DRM2 (J)	Decision quantity of raw material 2, Team J.
DRM3 (J)	Decision quantity of raw material 3, Team J.
DSEC (J)	Dollars to invest into short-term securities, Team J.
EINT (J)	Interest expense in $, Team J.
EQ (J)	Present equity position, Team J.
FXC (J)	Plant and equipment in $, Team J.
I	Period number.
IT	Number of teams.
IT2	Parameter variable--number of copies desired per team.
J	Team number.
L1	Index number computed to indicate the period number in the current cycle.
N	Number of operating periods.
OH (J)	Total overhead expenses, Team J.
OX (J)	Operating Expense, Team J.
Pas1 (J)	Product One available for sale, Team J.
PAS2 (J)	Product Two available for sale, Team J.
PEN (J)	Administrator penalty against Team J.
PD1 (J)	Demand for Product One, Team J.
PD2 (J)	Demand for Product Two, Team J.
POTD1	Unadjusted demand Product One, Team J.
POTD2	Unadjusted demand Product Two, Team J.
PR1 (J)	Price of Product One, Team J.
PR2 (J)	Price of Product Two, Team J.
PROF (J)	Traditional (absorption) accounting profits, Team J.
PROM (J)	Total production contribution, Team J.

VARIABLE NAME		VARIABLE DEFINITION
PROM1	(J)	Production contribution, Product One, Team J.
PROM2	(J)	Production contribution, Product Two, Team J.
PS1	(J)	Number of Product One sold, Team J.
PS2	(J)	Number of Product Two sold, Team J.
PSEC	(J)	Earnings from short-term securities, Team J.
PSU	(J)	Total product setup costs, Team J.
PSU1	(J)	Setup cost for Product One, Team J.
PSU2	(J)	Setup cost for Product Two, Team J.
PYMT	(J)	Payments to decrease debt, Team J.
Q		Current period number
QQ		Period number which is two periods ahead of the current period.
Q1		First coefficient for trend demand, Product One, Team J.
Q11		Second coefficient for trend demand, Product One, Team J.
Q2		First Coefficient for trend demand, Product Two, Team J.
Q22		Second coefficient for trend demand, Product Two, Team J.
QR1		Trend irregularities control parameter, Product One, Team J.
QR2		Trend irregularities control parameter, Product Two, Team J.
R		Percentage of current sales collected currently.
R1	(J)	Revenue from Product One, Team J.
R2	(J)	Revenue from Product Two, Team J.
RAN		Random variable generated by subroutine.
RANO		Random variable generated by subroutine and called in program.
RBO		Percentage of present stockout which is backordered for next period.
REBP1	(J)	Residual inventory of Product One, Team J.
REBP2	(J)	Residual inventory of Product Two, Team J.
RIM1	(J)	Actual units of raw materials 1 used in production, Team J.
RIM2	(J)	Actual units of raw materials 2 used in current production, Team J.
RIM3	(J)	Actual units of raw materials 3 used in current production, Team J.
RM1		Raw material 1 needed to produce Product Two.
RM2		Raw material 2 needed to produce Product One.
RM3		Raw material 3 needed to produce Product Two and Product One.
ROC	(J)	Total raw materials order costs, Team J.
ROC1	(J)	Raw material 1 order costs, Team J.
ROC2	(J)	Raw material 2 order costs, Team J.
ROC3	(J)	Raw material 3 order costs, Team J.
RPR1		Price of raw material 1.
RPR2		Price of raw material 2.
RPR3		Price of raw material 3.
RR		Random effective exchange ratio for materials 3, Team J.

VARIABLE NAME		VARIABLE DEFINITION
SEA		Seasonal effect for period I.
SK01	(J)	Stockout units of Product One, Team J.
SK02	(J)	Stockout units of Product Two, Team J.
SO11		Units to be deducted on next period caused by this period's stockout of Product One.
SO12		Units to be deducted in next period caused by last period's stockout of Product One.
SO21		Units to be deducted in next period caused by this period's stockout of Product Two.
SO22		Units to be deducted in next period caused by last period's stockout of Product Two.
TAST	(J)	Total assets, Team J.
TD12		Projected trend demand, Product One, period I+1.
TD13		Projected trend demand, Product One, period I+2.
TD22		Projected trend demand, Product Two, period I+1.
TD23		Projected trend demand, Product Two, period I+2.
TDC	(J)	Total overhead and operating expenses, Team J.
TMC	(J)	Total maintenance costs $[CML_{(J)} + XITM_{(J)}]$, Team J.
TR	(J)	Total revenue, Team J.
TRSEC	(J)	Total revenue from sales and securities, Team J.
TSEC	(J)	Total $ investment in short-term securities.
UCC1		Dollar carrying cost per unit of average inventory, Product One.
UCC2		Dollar carrying cost per unit of average inventory, Product Two.
URM1	(J)	Period unused units of raw materials 1, Team J.
URM2	(J)	Period unused units of raw materials 2, Team J.
URM3	(J)	Period unused units of raw materials 3, Team J.
VBF	(J)	Total inventory value of finished goods, Team J.
VBF1	(J)	Value beginning inventory finished goods, Product One, Team J.
VBF2	(J)	Value beginning inventory finished goods, Product Two, Team J.
VBRI	(J)	Total inventory value of raw materials, Team J.
VBRI1	(J)	Value of beginning raw material 1 inventory, Team J.
VBRI2	(J)	Value of beginning raw material 2 inventory, Team J.
VBRI3	(J)	Value of beginning raw material 3 inventory, Team J.
VREBP1	(J)	Value of residual inventory of Product One, Team J.
VREBP2	(J)	Value of residual inventory of Product Two, Team J.
XACR	(J)	Dummy variable for new accounts receivable.
XAVBF	(J)	Ending absorption value of finished goods, Team J.
XAVBF1	(J)	Ending absorption value of finished goods 1, Team J.
XAVBF2	(J)	Ending absorption value of finished goods 2, Team J.
XBIP1	(J)	Dummy variable to reserve beginning inventory Product One, Team J.

VARIABLE NAME	VARIABLE DEFINITION
XBIP2 (J)	Dummy variable to reserve beginning inventory Product Two, Team J.
XBRM1 (J)	Beginning raw material 1 used in producing Product One, Team J.
XBRM2 (J)	Beginning raw material 2 used in producing Product One, Team J.
XBRM3 (J)	Beginning raw material 3 used in producing Product One, Team J.
XC1 (J)	Capacity of machine 1 used in producing Product One, Team J.
XC2 (J)	Capacity of machine 2 used in producing Product One, Team J.
XC3 (J)	Capacity of machine 3 used in producing Product One, Team J.
XC4 (J)	Capacity of machine 4 used in producing Product One, Team J.
XCS (J)	Period ending cash position, Team J.
XDBT (J)	Period ending debt position, Team J.
XDLH (J)	Hours left after producing Product One, Team J.
XFXC (J)	Value of fixed assets, end of period I, Team J.
X1C1 (J)	Investment capacity machine 1, Team J.
X1C2 (J)	Investment capacity machine 2, Team J.
X1C3 (J)	Investment capacity machine 3, Team J.
X1C4 (J)	Investment capacity machine 4, Team J.
XINT	Interest rate parameter.
XITM (J)	Idle time of maintenance, Team J.
XJ	Number of periods up to the beginning of the present cycle.
XK1	Base maintenance expense ($1.00/hr.)
XLH	Labor hours used in producing Product One.
XMO (J)	Total direct manufacturing overhead, Team J.
XMO1 (J)	Direct manufacturing overhead, Product One, Team J.
XMO2 (J)	Direct manufacturing overhead, Product Two, Team J.
XMRT	Total hours machine run time.
XVBF (J)	Direct cost value of ending finished goods inventory, Team J.
XVBF1 (J)	Ending inventory at direct cost, Product One, Team J.
XVBF2 (J)	Ending inventory at direct cost, Product One, Team J.
XVBRI1(J)	Ending inventory at direct cost, raw materials 1, Team J.
XVBRI2(J)	Ending inventory at direct cost, raw materials 2, Team J.
XVBRI3(J)	Ending inventory at direct cost, raw materials 3, Team J.
XXL	Cost per labor hour.
Y (J)	Distribution expenses, Team J.
ZC1	Amount of capacity 1 used in producing Product One.
ZC2	Amount of capacity 2 used in producing Product One.
ZC3	Amount of capacity 3 used in producing Product One.
ZC4	Amount of capacity 4 used in producing Product One.

Appendix B

Fortran Program for the OPSIM Environment

```
C
C          OPSIM--DARDEN AND LUCAS--1968
C     OPERATIONS MANAGEMENT SIMULATION-COPYRIGHT 1968 APPLETON-CENTURY-CROFT
C
      DIMENSION CRM31(10),CRM32(10),URM1(10),URM2(10),URM3(10),XVBF(10),
     1XCS(10),PYMT(10),XACR(10),XDBT(10),DBT(10),EINT(10),DEP(10),XFXC(1
     20),ACDP1(10),ACDP2(10),ACDP(10),ACGAS1(10),ACGAS2(10),ACGAS(10),AD
     3MIN1(10),ADMIN2(10),ACG1(10),ACG2(10),ACG(10),AVBF1(10),AVBF2(10),
     4XAVBF1(10),XAVBF2(10),XAVBF(10),VBRI(10),TAST(10),EQ(10),APROM1(10
     5),APROM2(10),APROM(10),PROF(10),OX(10),AVBF(10),PSU1(10),PSU2(10)
      DIMENSION PROM1(10),PROM2(10),PROM(10),VBF(10),CLH1(10),CLH2(10),C
     1LH(10),XVBRI1(10),XVBRI2(10),XVBF1(10),XVBF2(10),CRM1(10),CRM2(10)
     2,CRM3(10),CRM(10),RIM1(10),RIM2(10),RIM3(10),CDP(10),CGAS1(10),CGA
     3S2(10),CGAS(10),ADMIN(10),TDC(10),CONOP(10),XVBRI3(10),ABR1(10),AB
     4R2(10),ABR3(10),CDP1(10),CDP2(10),CCRM1(10),CCRM2(10),CCRM3(10),RO
     5C1(10),ROC2(10),ROC3(10),ROC(10),COC(10),REBP1(10),VREBP1(10)
      DIMENSION REBP2(10),VREBP2(10),CG2(10),CG(10),CCP1(10),CCP2(10),CC
     1P(10),PSU(10),XITM(10),CML(10),TMC(10),Y(10),CG1(10),BIP1(10),BIP2
     2(10),BRM1(10),BRM2(10),BRM3(10),VBF1(10), VBF2(10),VBRI1(10),VBRI2
     3(10),VBRI3(10),C1(10),C2(10),C3(10),C4(10),CS2(10),CCG1(10),CCG2(1
     40),CMT(10),CCOC(10),CCSC(10),BO1(10),BO2(10),SO11(10),SO12(10),SO2
     51(10),SO22(10),CS1(10),CS(10),ACR(10),FXC(10)
      DIMENSION DP1(10),DP2(10),DRM1(10),DRM2(10),DRM3(10),DLH(10),DML(1
     10),XIC1(10),XIC2(10),XIC3(10),XIC4(10),XBRM1(10),XBRM2(10),XBRM3(1
     20),XDLH(10),PD1(10),PD2(10),PAS1(10),PAS2(10),PS1(10),PS2(10),SKO1
     3(10),SKO2(10),R1(10),R2(10),TR(10),XMO1(10),XMO2(10), XMO(10),XBIP
     41(10),XBIP2(10),XC1(10),XC2(10),XC3(10),XC4(10),TSEC(10),DSEC(10),
     5PSEC(10),TRSEC(10),PEN(10)
C     READ IN PARAMETER DECK
      READ1,IT,N,IT2,PR1,PR2,RPR1,RPR2,RPR3,XXL,BD,BD1,QR1,QR2,Q1,Q2,
     CQ11,Q22,  UCC1,UCC2,XINT,DIV,BEN
 1    FORMAT(3I3,2F3.0,4F4.2,2F2.0,2F3.2,4F5.0,2F3.2,3F4.3)
C     READ IN HISTORY DECK
      READ2,I,RAN
 2    FORMAT(I3,F12.0)
      DO1003J=1,IT
 1003 READ1004,BIP1(J),BIP2(J),BRM1(J),BRM2(J),BRM3(J),VBF1(J),VBF2(J),
     CVBRI1(J),VBRI2(J),VBRI3(J),C1(J),C2(J),C3(J),C4(J),CS1(J),CS2(J)
     C,CCG1(J),CCG2(J),CMT(J),CCOC(J),CCSC(J),BO1(J),BO2(J),SO11(J),SO12
     C(J),SO21(J),SO22(J),CS(J),ACR(J),FXC(J),DBT(J),AVBF1(J),AVBF2(J),
     CTSEC(J)
 1004 FORMAT(6X,2F11.0,4F12.0/6F12.0/6F12.0/6F12.0/6F12.0/4F12.0)
C     READ IN DECISION CARDS
      DO1005J=1,IT
 1005 READ3, DP1(J),DP2(J),DRM1(J),DRM2(J),DRM3(J),DLH(J),DML(J),XIC
     C1(J),XIC2(J),XIC3(J),XIC4(J),PYMT(J),DSEC(J),PEN(J)
 3    FORMAT(6X,2F7.0,3F8.0,F5.0,5F2.0,2F8.0,F5.0)
      DO999J=1,IT
C     CHECKING PRODUCTION DECISIONS
      XC2(J)=C2(J)
      XC4(J)=C4(J)
      CALL RANDOM(RANO,RAN)
      IF(RANO-BD )227,227,228
 227  IF(RANO-BD1)229,229,230
 229  XC2(J)=C2(J)-(500./(.25*DML(J)+1.))
```

```
        GOTO228                                                         0052
230     XC4(J)=C4(J)-900./(.35*DML(J)+1.0)                              0053
228     ZC1=70.0*DP1(J)/1000.0                                          0054
        IF(ZC1-C1(J))5,5,4                                              0055
4       DP1(J)=C1(J)*1000.0/70.0                                        0056
5       ZC2=25.0*DP1(J)/1000.0                                          0057
        IF(ZC2-XC2(J))7,7,6                                             0058
6       DP1(J)=XC2(J)*1000.0/25.0                                       0059
7       ZC3=25.0*DP1(J)/1000.0                                          0060
        IF(ZC3-C3(J))9,9,8                                              0061
8       DP1(J)=C3(J)*1000.0/25.0                                        0062
9       ZC4=30.0*DP1(J)/1000.0                                          0063
        IF(ZC4-XC4(J))11,11,10                                          0064
10      DP1(J)=XC4(J)*1000.0/30.0                                       0065
C       CHECK RAW MATERIALS                                             0066
11      RM2=40.0*DP1(J)                                                 0067
        IF(RM2-BRM2(J))13,13,12                                         0068
12      DP1(J)=BRM2(J)/40.0                                             0069
13      CALL RANDOM(RANO,RAN)                                           0070
        IF(RANO-4.)131,131,123                                          0071
123     IF(RANO-24.)132,132,124                                         0072
124     IF(RANO-74.)133,133,125                                         0073
125     IF(RANO-94.)134,134,135                                         0074
131     RR=9.0                                                          0075
        GOTO136                                                         0076
132     RR=9.5                                                          0077
        GOTO136                                                         0078
133     RR=10.0                                                         0079
        GOTO136                                                         0080
134     RR=10.5                                                         0081
        GOTO136                                                         0082
135     RR=11.0                                                         0083
136     RM3=DP1(J)*RR                                                   0084
        IF(RM3-BRM3(J))15,15,14                                         0085
14      DP1(J)=BRM3(J)/(1.0*RR)                                         0086
15      XLH=0.280*DP1(J)                                                0087
        IF(XLH-DLH(J))17,17,16                                          0088
16      DP1(J)=DLH(J)/0.280                                             0089
        XLH=0.280*DP1(J)                                                0090
C       REVISING CAPACITIES, INVENTORIES AND LABOR AVAILABLE            0091
17      XC1(J)=C1(J)-DP1(J)*70.0/1000.0                                 0092
        XC3(J)=C3(J)-DP1(J)*25.0/1000.0                                 0093
        XC4(J)=XC4(J)-DP1(J)*30.0/1000.0                                0094
        XBRM2(J)= BRM2(J)-DP1(J)*40.0                                   0095
        XBRM3(J)=BRM3(J)-RM3                                            0096
        XDLH(J)=DLH(J)-XLH                                              0097
C       THE DETERMINATION OF PRODUCT TWO THAT CAN BE PRODUCED           0098
        CC1=30.0*DP2(J)/1000.0                                          0099
        IF(CC1-XC1(J))19,19,18                                          0100
18      DP2(J)=XC1(J)*1000.0/30.0                                       0101
19      CC3=20.0*DP2(J)/1000.0                                          0102
        IF(CC3-XC3(J))21,21,20                                          0103
20      DP2(J)=XC3(J)*1000.0/20.0                                       0104
21      CC4=15.0*DP2(J)/1000.0                                          0105
        IF(CC4-XC4(J))23,23,22                                          0106
```

```
22    DP2(J)=XC4(J)*1000.0/15.0                                    0107
23    RM1=25.0*DP2(J)                                              0108
      IF(RM1-BRM1(J))25,25,24                                      0109
24    DP2(J)=BRM1(J)/25.0                                          0110
   25 RM3=DP2(J)*1.5*RR                                            0111
      IF(RM3-XBRM3(J))27,27,26                                     0112
   26 DP2(J)=XBRM3(J)/(1.5*RR)                                     0113
27    XLH=0.20*DP2(J)                                              0114
      IF(XLH-XDLH(J))29,29,28                                      0115
28    DP2(J)=XDLH(J)/0.20                                          0116
29    RM1=DP2(J)*25.0                                              0117
      RM2=DP1(J)*40.0                                              0118
      RM3=(DP1(J)+DP2(J)*1.5)*RR                                   0119
      RIM1(J)=RM1                                                  0120
      RIM2(J)=RM2                                                  0121
      RIM3(J)=RM3                                                  0122
      XBRM1(J)=BRM1(J)                                             0123
      XBRM2(J)=BRM2(J)                                             0124
      XBRM3(J)=BRM3(J)                                             0125
C     DETERMINATION OF SALES THIS PERIOD AND STOCKOUT EFFECTS      0126
      XJ=I/6                                                       0127
      XJ=XJ*6.                                                     0128
      Q=I                                                          0129
      L1=Q-XJ+1.                                                   0130
      GOTO(394,390,391,392,393,395),L1                            0131
  390 SEA=750.                                                     0132
      GOTO399                                                      0133
  391 SEA=1000.                                                    0134
      GOTO399                                                      0135
  392 SEA=250.                                                     0136
      GOTO399                                                      0137
  393 SEA=-625.                                                    0138
      GOTO399                                                      0139
  395 SEA=-750.                                                    0140
      GOTO399                                                      0141
  394 SEA=-625.                                                    0142
  399 CALL RANDOM(RANO,RAN)                                        0143
      IF(RANO-24.)1006,1006,1007                                   0144
 1007 IF(RANO-74.)1008,1008,1009                                   0145
 1006 POTD1=15000.+Q*Q1+(Q**2)*Q11-500.*QR1+SEA                    0146
      GOTO1010                                                     0147
 1008 POTD1=15000.+Q*Q1+(Q**2)*Q11+SEA                             0148
      GOTO1010                                                     0149
 1009 POTD1=15000.+Q*Q1+(Q**2)*Q11+500.*QR1+SEA                    0150
 1010 CALL RANDOM(RANO,RAN)                                        0151
      IF(RANO-24.)1011,1011,1012                                   0152
 1012 IF(RANO-74.)1013,1013,1014                                   0153
 1011 POTD2=19500.+Q*Q2+(Q**2)*Q22-1000.*QR2                       0154
      GOTO1015                                                     0155
 1013 POTD2=19500.+Q*Q2+(Q**2)*Q22                                 0156
      GOTO1015                                                     0157
 1014 POTD2=19500.+Q*Q2+(Q**2)*Q22+1000.*QR2                       0158
 1015 PD1(J)=POTD1+BO1(J)-SO11(J)-SO12(J)                          0159
      PD2(J)=POTD2+BO2(J)-SO21(J)-SO22(J)                          0160
      PAS1(J)=BIP1(J)+DP1(J)                                       0161
```

```
      PAS2(J)=BIP2(J)+DP2(J)                                     0162
      IF(PAS1(J)-PD1(J))30,30,31                                 0163
   30 PS1(J)=PAS1(J)                                             0164
      SKO1(J)=(PD1(J)-PAS1(J))                                   0165
      GO TO 32                                                   0166
   31 PS1(J)=PD1(J)                                              0167
      SKO1(J)=0.0                                                0168
   32 IF(PAS2(J)-PD2(J))33,33,34                                 0169
   33 PS2(J)=PAS2(J)                                             0170
      SKO2(J)=(PD2(J)-PAS2(J))                                   0171
      GO TO 35                                                   0172
   34 PS2(J)=PD2(J)                                              0173
      SKO2(J)=0.0                                                0174
   35 R1(J)=PR1    *PS1(J)                                       0175
      R2(J)=PR2    *PS2(J)                                       0176
      TR(J)=R1(J)+R2(J)                                          0177
C     REVISING BACKORDERS AND STOCKOUTS FOR HISTORY             0178
      CALL RANDOM(RANO,RAN)                                      0179
      IF(RANO-4.)115,115,114                                     0180
  114 IF(RANO-24.)116,116,117                                    0181
  117 IF(RANO-74.)118,118,119                                    0182
  119 IF(RANO-94.)120,120,121                                    0183
  115 RBO=.70                                                    0184
      GOTO122                                                    0185
  116 RBO=.75                                                    0186
      GOTO122                                                    0187
  118 RBO=.80                                                    0188
      GOTO122                                                    0189
  120 RBO=.85                                                    0190
      GOTO122                                                    0191
  121 RBO=.90                                                    0192
  122 BO1(J)=RBO*SKO1(J)                                         0193
      BO2(J)=RBO*SKO2(J)                                         0194
      SO12(J)=0.5*SO11(J)                                        0195
      SO11(J)=0.5*SKO1(J)                                        0196
      SO22(J)=0.5*SO21(J)                                        0197
      SO21(J)=0.5*SKO2(J)                                        0198
C     DETERMINATION OF DIRECT MFG OVERHEAD                       0199
      XMO1(J)=DP1(J)*0.07+BEN*DP1(J)                             0200
      XMO2(J)=DP2(J)*0.05 +BEN*DP2(J)                            0201
      XMO(J)=XMO1(J) + XMO2(J)                                   0202
C     NEXT PERIODS RAW MATERIAL VALUES                          0203
      ABR1(J)=VBRI1(J)/BRM1(J)                                   0204
      ABR2(J)=VBRI2(J)/BRM2(J)                                   0205
      ABR3(J)=VBRI3(J)/BRM3(J)                                   0206
      CRM1(J)=RM1*ABR1(J)                                        0207
      CRM2(J)=RM2*ABR2(J)                                        0208
      CRM3(J)=RM3*ABR3(J)                                        0209
      CRM31(J)=DP1(J)*ABR3(J)*RR                                 0210
      CRM32(J)=DP2(J)*ABR3(J)*1.5*RR                             0211
      CRM(J)=CRM1(J)+CRM2(J)+CRM3(J)                             0212
      XVBRI1(J)=VBRI1(J)                                         0213
      XVBRI2(J)=VBRI2(J)                                         0214
      XVBRI3(J)=VBRI3(J)                                         0215
      VBRI1(J)=(BRM1(J)-RM1)*ABR1(J)+DRM1(J)*RPR1                0216
```

```
      VBRI2(J)=(BRM2(J)-RM2)*ABR2(J)+DRM2(J)*RPR2                          0217
      VBRI3(J)=(BRM3(J)-RM3)*ABR3(J)+DRM3(J)*RPR3                          0218
C     COMPUTE COST OF GOODS PRODUCED IN CURRENT PERIOD                     0219
      CLH1(J)=XXL*DP1(J)*.28                                               0220
      CLH2(J)=XXL*DP2(J)*.20                                               0221
      CDP1(J)=CLH1(J)+DP1(J)*(40.*ABR2(J)+ABR3(J)*RR)+XMO1(J)             0222
      CDP2(J)=CLH2(J)+DP2(J)*(25.*ABR1(J)+1.5*ABR3(J)*RR)+XMO2(J)         0223
      CDP(J)=CDP1(J)+CDP2(J)                                               0224
      CLH(J)=CLH1(J)+CLH2(J)                                               0225
C     RAW MATERIALS CARRYING COST COMPUTATIONS                             0226
      CCRM1(J)=.050*(2.0*BRM1(J)-RM1)                                      0227
      CCRM2(J)=.055*(2.0*BRM2(J)-RM2)                                      0228
      CCRM3(J)=.045*(2.0*BRM3(J)-RM3)                                      0229
C     ORDER COST DETERMINATION                                             0230
      IF(DRM1(J))40,40,41                                                  0231
   40 ROC1(J)=0.0                                                          0232
      GO TO 53                                                             0233
   41 ROC1(J)=1500.0                                                       0234
   53 IF(DRM2(J))42,42,43                                                  0235
   42 ROC2(J)=0.0                                                          0236
      GOTO54                                                               0237
   43 ROC2(J)=2000.0                                                       0238
   54 IF(DRM3(J))51,51,52                                                  0239
   51 ROC3(J)=0.0                                                          0240
      GOTO55                                                               0241
   52 ROC3(J)=2000.0                                                       0242
   55 ROC(J)=ROC1(J)+ ROC2(J)+ROC3(J)                                      0243
      COC(J)=CCRM1(J)+CCRM2(J)+CCRM3(J)+ROC(J)                            0244
C     REDEFINING COMPUTATION OF NEW RAW MATERIALS INVENTORIES             0245
      URM1(J)=BRM1(J)-RM1                                                  0246
      URM2(J)=BRM2(J)-RM2                                                  0247
      URM3(J)=BRM3(J)-RM3                                                  0248
      BRM1(J)=URM1(J)+DRM1(J)                                              0249
      BRM2(J)=URM2(J)+DRM2(J)                                              0250
      BRM3(J)=URM3(J)+DRM3(J)                                              0251
C     DETERMINATION OF COST OF GOODS SOLD AND NEXT PERIOD INVENTCRIES     0252
      XVBF1(J)=VBF1(J)                                                     0253
      XVBF2(J)=VBF2(J)                                                     0254
      XVBF(J)=XVBF1(J)+XVBF2(J)                                            0255
      XBIP1(J)=BIP1(J)                                                     0256
      XBIP2(J)=BIP2(J)                                                     0257
      IF(PS1(J)-BIP1(J))36,36,37                                          0258
   36 REBP1(J)=BIP1(J)-PS1(J)                                             0259
      CG1(J)=PS1(J)*(VBF1(J)/BIP1(J))                                     0260
      VREBP1(J)=REBP1(J)*VBF1(J)/BIP1(J)                                  0261
      BIP1(J)=REBP1(J)+DP1(J)                                             0262
      VBF1(J)=VREBP1(J)+CDP1(J)                                           0263
      GOTO38                                                              0264
   37 CG1(J)=VBF1(J)+(CDP1(J)/DP1(J))*(PS1(J)-BIP1(J))                    0265
      VBF1(J)=((BIP1(J)+DP1(J))-PS1(J))*(CDP1(J)/DP1(J))                  0266
      BIP1(J)=DP1(J)+BIP1(J)-PS1(J)                                       0267
   38 IF(PS2(J)-BIP2(J))39,39,60                                          0268
   39 REBP2(J)=BIP2(J)-PS2(J)                                             0269
      VREBP2(J)=REBP2(J)*VBF2(J)/BIP2(J)                                  0270
   84 CG2(J)=PS2(J)* VBF2(J)/BIP2(J)                                      0271
```

```
      BIP2(J)=REBP2(J)+DP2(J)                                              0272
      VBF2(J)=VREBP2(J)+CDP2(J)                                           0273
      GOTO61                                                              0274
  60  CG2(J)=VBF2(J)+(CDP2(J)/DP2(J))*(PS2(J)-BIP2(J))                    0275
      VBF2(J)=((BIP2(J)+DP2(J))-PS2(J))*CDP2(J)/DP2(J)                    0276
      BIP2(J)=DP2(J)+BIP2(J)-PS2(J)                                       0277
  61  VBF(J)=VBF1(J)+VBF2(J)                                              0278
      CG(J)=CG1(J)+CG2(J)                                                 0279
      CGAS1(J)=CDP1(J)+XVBF1(J)                                           0280
      CGAS2(J)=CDP2(J)+XVBF2(J)                                           0281
      CGAS(J)=CGAS1(J)+CGAS2(J)                                           0282
C     COMPUTATION OF FINISHED GOODS CARRYING COSTS                        0283
      CCP1(J)=UCC1*(BIP1(J)+XBIP1(J))/2.0                                 0284
      CCP2(J)=UCC2*(BIP2(J)+XBIP2(J))/2.0                                 0285
      CCP(J)=CCP1(J)+CCP2(J)                                              0286
C     SETUP COST FOR FINISHED PRODUCT                                     0287
      IF(DP1(J))44,44,45                                                  0288
  44  PSU1(J)=0.0                                                         0289
      GO TO 88                                                            0290
  45  PSU1(J)=5000.                                                       0291
  88  IF(DP2(J))46,46,47                                                  0292
  46  PSU2(J)=0.0                                                         0293
      GO TO 89                                                            0294
  47  PSU2(J)=6000.                                                       0295
  89  PSU(J)=PSU1(J)+PSU2(J)                                              0296
C     COMPUTATION OF MAINTENANCE EXPENSE                                  0297
      XK1=DP1(J)*.150+DP2(J)*.065                                         0298
      IF(DML(J))48,48,49                                                  0299
  48  XITM(J)=XK1+2500.0                                                  0300
      GOTO50                                                              0301
  49  XITM(J)=XK1+(1500.0/DML(J))                                         0302
  50  CML(J)=500.0*DML(J)                                                 0303
      TMC(J)=CML(J)+XITM(J)                                               0304
C     DETERMINATION OF PLANT CAPACITY INVESTMENT FOR NEXT PERIOD          0305
      XC1(J)=C1(J)+XIC1(J)*2100.0                                         0306
      XC2(J)=C2(J)+XIC2(J)*500.0                                          0307
      XC3(J)=C3(J)+XIC3(J)*1000.0                                         0308
      XC4(J)=C4(J)+XIC4(J)*900.0                                          0309
C     COMPUTATION OF CUMULATIVE TOTALS                                    0310
      CCG1(J)=CCG1(J)+CG1(J)                                              0311
      CCG2(J)=CCG2(J)+CG2(J)                                              0312
      CS1(J)=CS1(J)+R1(J)                                                 0313
      CS2(J)=CS2(J)+R2(J)                                                 0314
      CMT(J)=CMT(J)+XITM(J)                                               0315
      CCSC(J)=CCSC(J)+PSU(J)+CCP(J)                                       0316
      CCOC(J)=CCOC(J)+COC(J)                                              0317
C     COMPUTATION OF ADMINISTRATIVE COST                                 0318
      ADMIN(J)=200000.+2.5*DP1(J)+2.0*DP2(J)+COC(J)+PSU(J)+TMC(J)+XXL*DL  0319
     1H(J)-CLH(J)                                                         0320
C     COMPUTATION OF MARKETING AND DISTRIBUTION EXPENSES                 0321
      Y(J)=300000.+POTD1*3.0+POTD2*3.6+PS1(J)*2.0+PS2(J)*2.4+CCP(J)       0322
      TDC(J)=ADMIN(J)+Y(J)                                                0323
      PROM1(J)=R1(J)-CG1(J)                                               0324
      PROM2(J)=R2(J)-CG2(J)                                               0325
      IF(TSEC(J)+DSEC(J))1016,1017,1017                                   0326
```

```
 1016 DSEC(J)=-TSEC(J)
 1017 TSEC(J)=TSEC(J)+DSEC(J)
      PSEC(J)=TSEC(J)*DIV
      TRSEC(J)=TR(J)+PSEC(J)
      PROM(J)=TRSEC(J)-CG(J)
C     NEW CASH FLOWS
      CALL RANDOM(RANO,RAN)
      IF(RANO-29.)96,96,95
 95   IF(RANO-69.)97,97,98
 96   R=0.70
      GO TO 99
 97   R=0.75
      GO TO 99
 98   R=0.80
 99   XDBT(J)=DBT(J)-PYMT(J)+100000.*(XIC2(J)+XIC4(J))+150000.*(XIC1(J)+
     1XIC3(J))
      IF(XDBT(J))225,226,226
  225 PYMT(J)=PYMT(J)+XDBT(J)
      XDBT(J)=0.0
  226 EINT(J)=XDBT(J)*XINT
      XCS(J)=CS(J)+R*TR(J)-TDC(J)+ACR(J)-PYMT(J)-AINT(J)-CLH(J)-DRM1(J)*
     2RPR1-DRM2(J)*RPR2-DRM3(J)*RPR3-XMO(J)-DSEC(J)+PSEC(J)
C     CHECK FOR NEW DEBT
      XACR(J)=(1.0-R)*TR(J)
C     INTEREST AND DEBT ADJUSTMENTS
      IF(XCS(J))100,111,111
 100  XDBT(J)=XDBT(J)-XCS(J)-XINT*XCS(J)
      EINT(J)=EINT(J)-XCS(J)*XINT
      XCS(J)=0.0
C     DEPRECIATION COMPUTATIONS
 111  DEP(J)=5000.+15.*(C1(J)/21.+C3(J)/10.)+10.*(C2(J)/5.+C4(J)/9.)
      XFXC(J)=FXC(J)-DEP(J)+150000.*(XIC1(J)+XIC3(J))+100000.*(XIC2(J)+X
     1IC4(J))
C     COMPUTATION OF ABSORPTION INVENTORY VALUES
      ADMIN(J)=ADMIN(J)+DEP(J)+PEN(J)
      TDC(J)=TDC(J)+DEP(J) +EINT(J)
      CONOP(J)=PROM(J)-TDC(J)
      ADMIN1(J)=ADMIN(J)*((DP1(J)+1.)/(DP1(J)+DP2(J)+2.))
      ADMIN2(J)=ADMIN(J)-ADMIN1(J)
      ACDP1(J)=CDP1(J)+ADMIN1(J)
      ACDP2(J)=CDP2(J)+ADMIN2(J)
      ACDP(J)=ACDP1(J)+ACDP2(J)
      ACGAS1(J)=AVBF1(J)+ACDP1(J)
      ACGAS2(J)=AVBF2(J)+ACDP2(J)
      ACGAS(J)=ACGAS1(J)+ACGAS2(J)
      IF(PS1(J)-XBIP1(J))101,101,102
 101  ACG1(J)=PS1(J)*AVBF1(J)/XBIP1(J)
      GO TO 103
 102  ACG1(J)=AVBF1(J)+(PS1(J)-XBIP1(J))*ACDP1(J)/DP1(J)
 103  IF(PS2(J)-XBIP2(J))104,104,105
 104  ACG2(J)=PS2(J)*AVBF2(J)/XBIP2(J)
      GOTO106
 105  ACG2(J)=AVBF2(J)+(PS2(J)-XBIP2(J))*ACDP2(J)/DP2(J)
 106  ACG(J)=ACG1(J)+ACG2(J)
      AVBF(J)=AVBF1(J)+AVBF2(J)
```

```
      XAVBF1(J)=ACGAS1(J)-ACG1(J)                                          0382
      XAVBF2(J)=ACGAS2(J)-ACG2(J)                                          0383
      XAVBF(J)=XAVBF1(J)+XAVBF2(J)                                         0384
      VBRI(J)=VBRI1(J)+VBRI2(J)+VBRI3(J)                                   0385
      TAST(J)=XCS(J)+XACR(J)+XAVBF(J)+VBRI(J)+XFXC(J)+TSEC(J)              0386
      EQ(J)=TAST(J)-XDBT(J)                                                0387
      APROM1(J)=R1(J)-ACG1(J)                                             0388
      APROM2(J)=R2(J)-ACG2(J)                                             0389
      APROM(J)=APROM1(J)+APROM2(J)+PSEC(J)                                 0390
      PROF(J)=APROM(J)-Y(J)-EINT(J)                                        0391
  999 OX(J)=EINT(J)+Y(J)                                                   0392
      Q=I+1                                                                0393
      QQ=Q+1.                                                              0394
      TD12=15000.+Q*Q1+(Q**2)*Q11                                          0395
      TD22=19500.+Q*Q2 +(Q**2)*Q22                                         0396
      TD13=15000.+QQ*Q1+(QQ**2)*Q11                                        0397
      TD23=19500.+QQ*Q2 +(QQ**2)*Q22                                       0398
      DO139J=1,IT                                                          0399
      DO139I9=1,IT2                                                        0400
      PRINT90,I,J                                                          0401
   90 FORMAT(1H1,44X,32HOPERATIONS MANAGEMENT SIMULATION////10X,6HPERIOD   0402
     1,I3//37X,31HMANAGERIAL OPERATIONS STATEMENT/5X,4HFIRM,I3//55X,5HUN   0403
     2ITS,2X,11HPRODUCT ONE,1X,11HPRODUCT TWO,6X,6HTOTALS/)               0404
   91 PRINT92,R1(J),R2(J),TR(J),PSEC(J),TRSEC(J),XVBF1(J),XVBF2(J),XVBF(   0406
     2J),CLH1(J),CLH2(J),CLH(J),RIM1(J),CRM1(J),CRM1(J),RIM2(J),CRM2(J),   0407
     3CRM2(J),RIM3(J),CRM31(J),CRM32(J),CRM3(J),CRM(J),XMO1(J),XMO2(J),X   0408
     4MO(J),CDP1(J),CDP2(J),CDP(J)                                         0409
   92 FORMAT(1H ,9X,5HSALES,47X,3F12.0/15X,12HOTHER INCOME,F71.0/20X,      0410
     112HTOTAL INCOME,54X,F12.0/10X,32HLESS VARIABLE COST OF GOODS SOLD/   0411
     213X,34HBEGINNING INVENTORY-FINISHED GOODS,15X,3F12.0/13X,18HCURREN   0412
     3T PRODUCTION/16X,12HDIRECT LABOR,34X,3F12.0/16X,16HDIRECT MATERIAL   0413
     4S/19X,22HRAW MATERIALS ONE USED,9X,F12.0,12X,2F12.0/19X,22HRAW MAT   0414
     5ERIALS TWO USED,9X,2F12.0,12X,F12.0/19X,24HRAW MATERIALS THREE USE   0415
     6D,7X,4F12.0//20X,27HTOTAL DIRECT MATERIALS COST,39X,F12.0//16X,17H   0416
     7VARIABLE OVERHEAD,29X,3F12.0//13X,31HCOST OF CURRENT PRODUCTION(VA   0417
     8R),18X,3F12.0//)                                                     0418
      PRINT93,CGAS1(J),CGAS2(J),CGAS(J),VBF1(J),VBF2(J),VBF(J),CG1(J),CG   0419
     12(J),CG(J),PROM1(J),PROM2(J),PROM(J),Y(J),ADMIN(J),EINT(J),TDC(J),   0420
     2CONOP(J)                                                             0421
   93 FORMAT(13X,21HTOTAL GOODS AVAILABLE,28X,3F12.0/13X,21HLESS ENDING    0422
     1INVENTORY,28X,3F12.0//13X,27HVARIABLE COST OF GOODS SOLD,22X,3F12.   0423
     20//13X,26HVARIABLE PRODUCTION MARGIN,23X,3F12.0//10X,28HLESS ADDIT   0424
     3IONAL PERIOD COSTS/16X,27HSELLING AND ADMIN. EXPENSES,43X,F12.0/16   0425
     4X,8HOVERHEAD,62X,F12.0/16X,8HINTEREST,62X,F12.0/13X,23HADDITIONAL    0426
     5PERIOD COSTS,50X,F12.0//10X,28HCONTRIBUTION FROM OPERATIONS,48X,F1   0427
     62.0//)                                                               0428
      PRINT107,I,J,XDBT(J),XCS(J),XACR(J),EQ(J),TSEC(J),XAVBF1(J),XAVBF2   0429
     1(J),XAVBF(J),VBRI1(J),VBRI2(J),VBRI3(J),VBRI(J),XFXC(J),TAST(J),TA   0430
     2ST(J)                                                                0431
  107 FORMAT(1H1,44X,6HPERIOD,I3,15H   BALANCE SHEET///5X,4HFIRM,I3//15X,  0432
     16HASSETS,44X,11HLIABILITIES//5X,14HCURRENT ASSETS,36X,4HDEBT,35X,F   0433
     210.0/8X,4HCASH,28X,F10.0/8X,19HACCOUNTS RECEIVABLE,13X,F10.0,5X,13   0434
     3HOWNERS EQUITY,26X,F10.0/8X,21HSHORT TERM SECURITIES,11X,F10.0/8X,   0435
     49HINVENTORY/11X,14HFINISHED GOODS/13X,11HPRODUCT ONE,6X,F10.0/13X,   0436
     511HPRODUCT TWO,6X,F10.0/15X,5HTOTAL,20X,F10.0/11X,13HRAW MATERIALS   0437
```

```
      6/14X,13HMATERIALS ONE,3X,F10.0/14X,12HMATERIAL TWO,4X,F10.0/14X,14
      7HMATERIAL THREE,2X,F10.0/15X,5HTOTAL,20X,F10.0//5X,19HPLANT AND EQ
      8UIPMENT,16X,F10.0///9X,12HTOTAL ASSETS,19X,F10.0,9X,28HTOTAL LIABI
      9LITIES AND EQUITY,7X,F10.0///)
       PRINT108,I,J
108    FORMAT(1H1,44X,6HPERIOD,I3,29H  ABSORPTION INCOME STATEMENT///5X,4
      1HFIRM,I3//63X,11HPRODUCT ONE,1X,11HPRODUCT TWO,4X,6HTOTALS//)
       PRINT109,R1(J),R2(J),TR(J),PSEC(J),TRSEC(J),AVBF1(J),AVBF2(J),AVBF
      1(J),CLH1(J),CLH2(J),CLH(J),CRM1(J),CRM1(J),CRM2(J),CRM2(J),CRM31(J
      2),CRM32(J),CRM3(J),XMO1(J),XMO2(J),XMO(J),ADMIN1(J),ADMIN2(J),ADMI
      3N(J),ACDP1(J),ACDP2(J),ACDP(J),ACGAS1(J),ACGAS2(J),ACGAS(J),XAVBF1
      4(J),XAVBF2(J),XAVBF(J),ACG1(J),ACG2(J),ACG(J)
109    FORMAT (10X,5HSALES,47X,3F12.0/15X,12HOTHER INCOME,59X,F12.0/20X,1
      12HTOTAL INCOME,54X,F12.0//10X,23HLESS COST OF GOODS SOLD/13X, 34HB
      2EGINNING INVENTORY-FINISHED GOODS,15X,3F12.0/13X,18HCURRENT PRODUC
      3TION/16X,12HDIRECT LABOR,34X,3F12.0/16X,16HDIRECT MATERIALS/19X,1
      47HRAW MATERIALS ONE,38X,2F12.0/19X,17HRAW MATERIALS TWO,F38.0,F24.
      50/   19X,19HRAW MATERIALS THREE,24X,3F12.0/16X,17HVARIABLE OVERHEA
      6D,29X,3F12.0/16X,24HOTHER ALLOCATED OVERHEAD,22X,3F12.0//16X,26HCO
      7ST OF CURRENT PRODUCTION,20X,3F12.0//13X,24HGOODS AVAILABLE FOR SA
      8LE,25X,3F12.0/13X,21HLESS ENDING INVENTORY,28X,3F12.0//10X,18HCOST
      9 OF GOODS SOLD,34X,3F12.0//)
       PRINT113,APROM1(J),APROM2(J),APROM(J),Y(J),EINT(J),OX(J),PROF(J)
 113   FORMAT(10X,23HPRODUCTION CONTRIBUTION,29X,3F12.0//10X,18HOPERATING
      1 EXPENSES/13X,29HMARKETING AND ADMIN. EXPENSES,44X,F12.0/13X,17HIN
      2TEREST PAYMENTS,56X,F12.0/16X,24HTOTAL OPERATING EXPENSES,46X,F12.
      30//10X,19HPROFIT BEFORE TAXES,57X,F12.0)
       PRINT110,J,XBIP1(J),XBIP2(J),XBRM1(J),XBRM2(J),XBRM3(J),DP1(J),DP
      12(J),RIM1(J),RIM2(J),RIM3(J),PAS1(J),PAS2(J),URM1(J),URM2(J),URM3(
      2J),PS1(J),PS2(J),DRM1(J),DRM2(J),DRM3(J),BIP1(J),BIP2(J),BRM1(J),B
      3RM2(J),BRM3(J)
110    FORMAT(1H1,51X,39HACCOUNTING INFORMATION (PHYSICAL UNITS)///5X,4HF
      1IRM,I3//17X,26HFINISHED GOODS INVENTORIES,34X,25HRAW MATERIALS INV
      2ENTORIES//30X,11HPRODUCT ONE,4X,11HPRODUCT TWO,27X,42HMATERIAL ONE
      3  MATERIAL TWO  MATERIAL THREE//5X,19HBEGINNING INVENTORY,6X,F11.0
      4,4X,F11.0,4X,19HBEGINNING INVENTORY,5X,2F11.0,F14.0/5X,23HPLUS CUR
      5RENT PRODUCTION,2X,F11.0,4X,F11.0,4X,19HLESS MATERIALS USED,5X,2F1
      61.0,F14.0//5X,24HGOODS AVAILABLE FOR SALE,1X,F11.0,4X,F11.0,4X,16H
      7UNUSED MATERIALS,8X,2F11.0,F14.0/5X,18HLESS CURRENT SALES,7X,F11.0
      8,4X,F11.0,4X,19HPLUS CURRENT ORDERS,5X,2F11.0,F14.0/5X,16HENDING I
      9NVENTORY,9X,F11.0,4X,F11.0,4X,16HENDING INVENTORY,8X,2F11.0,F14.0)
94     PRINT 137,CCP1(J),CCP2(J),CCRM1(J),CCRM2(J),CCRM3(J),PSU1(J),PSU2(
      1J),ROC1(J),ROC2(J),ROC3(J),I,PR1,PR2,RPR1,RPR2,RPR3,I,PD1(J),PD2(J
      2),Q,TD12,TD22,QQ,TD13,TD23
137    FORMAT(5X,13HCARRYING COST,12X,F11.0,4X,F11.0,28X,2F11.0,F14.0/5X,
      110HSETUP COST,15X,F11.0,4X,F11.0,28X,2F11.0,F14.0/5X,17HUNIT PRICE
      2 PERIOD,I3,5X,F11.0,4X,F11.0,28X,2F11.2,F14.2/5X,21HPRODUCT DEMAND
      3 PERIOD,I3,1X,F11.0,4X,F11.0/5X,21HPRODUCT DEMAND PERIOD,F4.0,1X,F
      410.0,4X,F11.0/5X,21HPRODUCT DEMAND PERIOD,F4.0,1X,F10.0,4X,F11.0)
       PRINT138
138    FORMAT(1H1,45X,15HINDUSTRY REPORT//40X,13H CONTRIBUTION,5X,6HEQUIT
      1Y,6X,6HPROFIT)
       DO139JK=1,IT
139    PRINT140,JK,CONOP(JK),EQ(JK),PROF(JK)
140    FORMAT(1H ,32X,4HTEAM,I2,4X,3F11.0)
```

```
C      PUNCH NEW HISTORY CARDS                                          0493
       I=I+1                                                            0494
       PUNCH2,I,RAN                                                     0495
       DO911J=1,IT                                                      0496
 911   PUNCH1004,BIP1(J),BIP2(J),BRM1(J),BRM2(J),BRM3(J),VBF1(J),VBF2(J), 0497
      1VBRI1(J),VBRI2(J),VBRI3(J),XC1(J),XC2(J),XC3(J),XC4(J),CS1(J),CS2( 0498
      1J),CCG1(J),CCG2(J),CMT(J),CCOC(J),CCSC(J),BO1(J),BO2(J),SO11(J),SO 0499
      212(J),SO21(J),SO22(J),XCS(J),XACR(J),XFXC(J),XDBT(J),XAVBF1(J),XAV 0500
      3BF2(J),TSEC(J)                                                   0501
       STOP                                                             0502
       END                                                              0503
       SUBROUTINE RANDOM(RANO,RAN)                                      0504
       RANX=RAN*23.0                                                    0505
       IRAN=RANX/(10.**8)                                               0506
       IRUN=RANX                                                        0507
       IRAV=IRUN-(IRAN*10**8)                                           0508
       RANY=IRAV-IRAN                                                   0509
       IRAY=RANY/(10.**3)                                               0510
       IRAX=(IRAY/100)*100                                              0511
       RANO=IRAY-IRAX                                                   0512
       RAN=RANY                                                         0513
       RETURN                                                           0514
       END                                                              0515
```

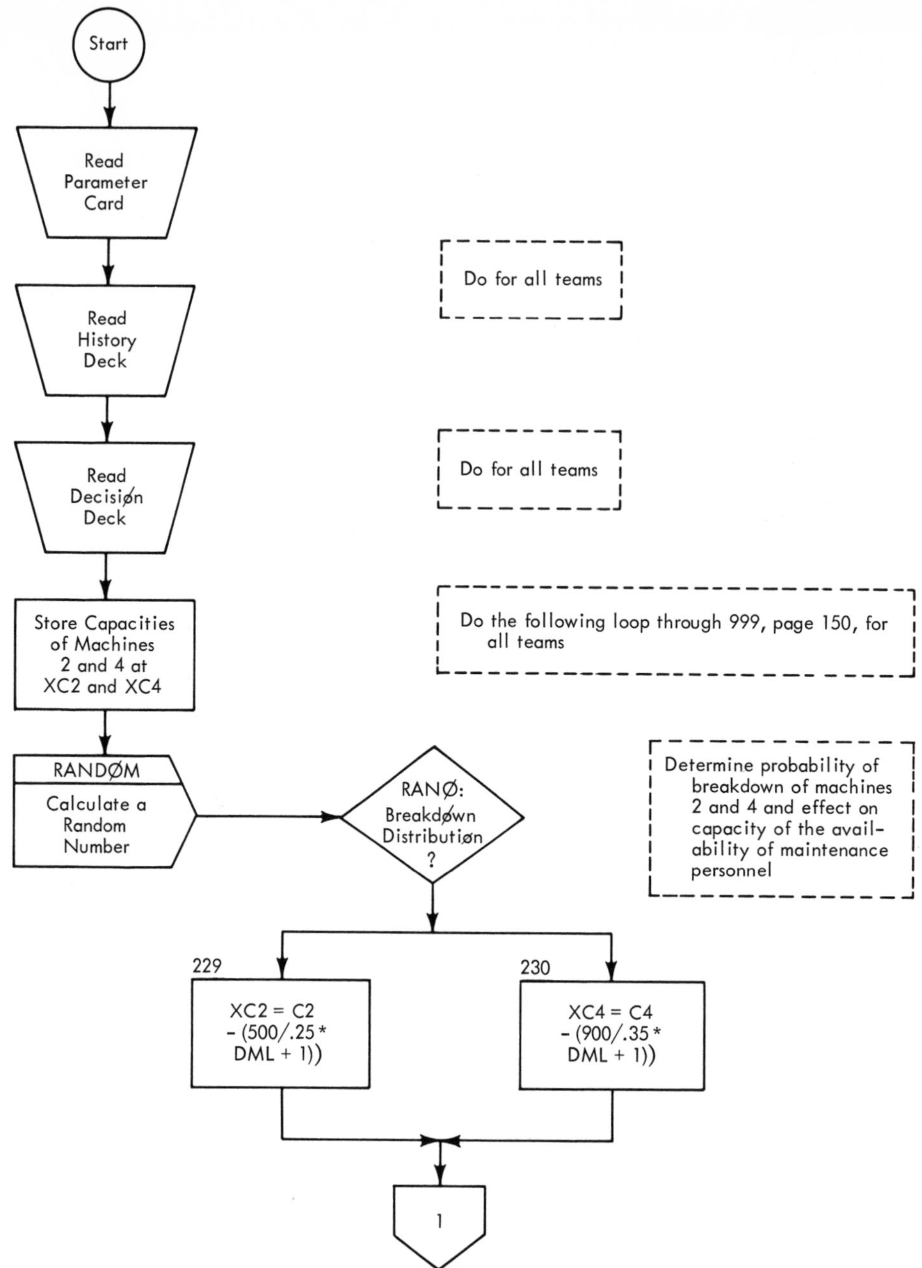

Start
Read Parameter Card
Read History Deck
Read Decisiøn Deck
Store Capacities of Machines 2 and 4 at XC2 and XC4
RANDØM
Calculate a Random Number
RANØ: Breakdøwn Distributiøn ?
229
XC2 = C2 - (500/.25* DML + 1))
230
XC4 = C4 - (900/.35* DML + 1))
1
Do for all teams
Do for all teams
Do the following loop through 999, page 150, for all teams
Determine probability of breakdown of machines 2 and 4 and effect on capacity of the availability of maintenance personnel

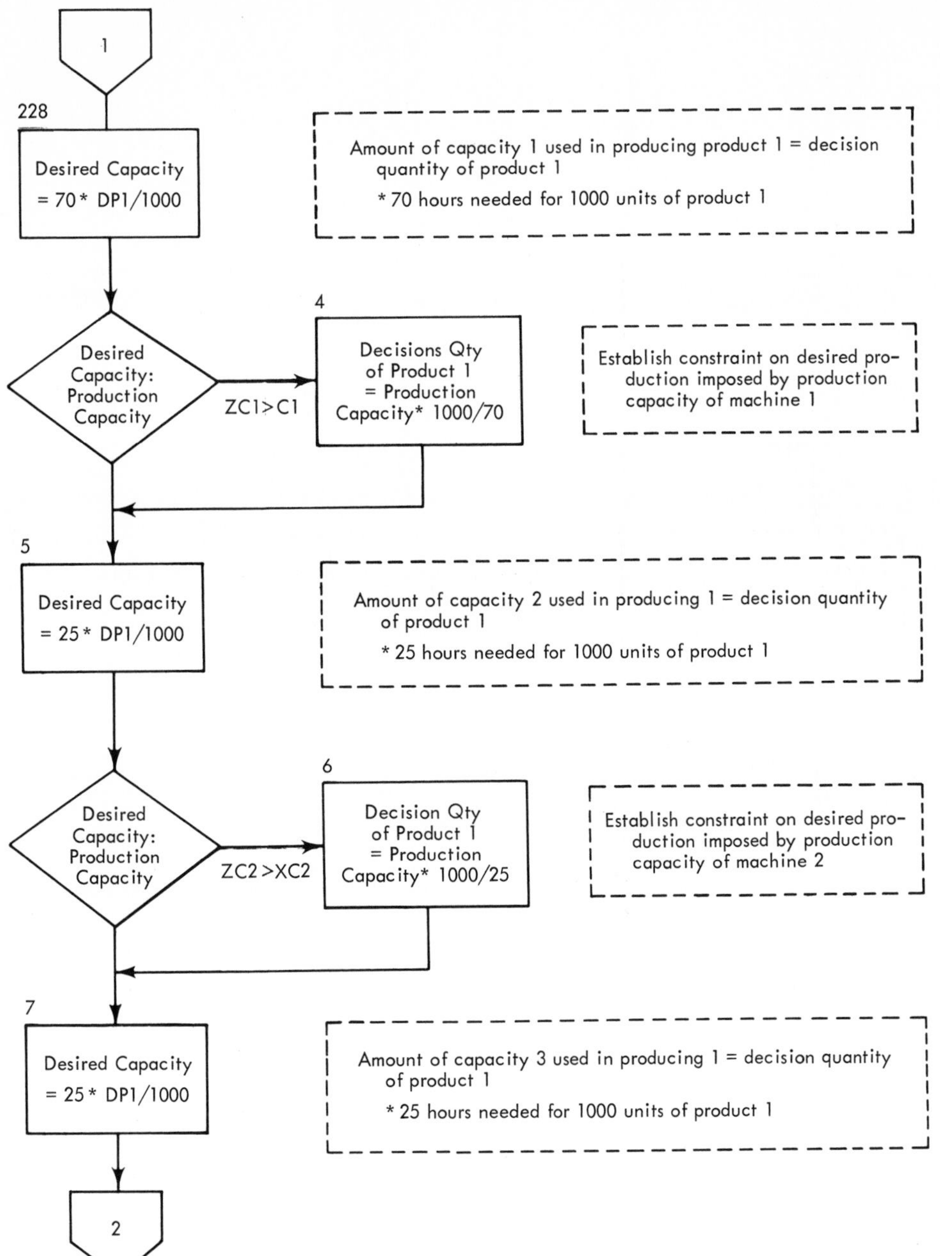
1
228
Desired Capacity
= 70* DP1/1000
Amount of capacity 1 used in producing product 1 = decision quantity of product 1
* 70 hours needed for 1000 units of product 1
Desired Capacity: Production Capacity
4
ZC1>C1
Decisions Qty of Product 1 = Production Capacity* 1000/70
Establish constraint on desired production imposed by production capacity of machine 1
5
Desired Capacity
= 25* DP1/1000
Amount of capacity 2 used in producing 1 = decision quantity of product 1
* 25 hours needed for 1000 units of product 1
Desired Capacity: Production Capacity
6
ZC2>XC2
Decision Qty of Product 1 = Production Capacity* 1000/25
Establish constraint on desired production imposed by production capacity of machine 2
7
Desired Capacity
= 25* DP1/1000
Amount of capacity 3 used in producing 1 = decision quantity of product 1
* 25 hours needed for 1000 units of product 1
2

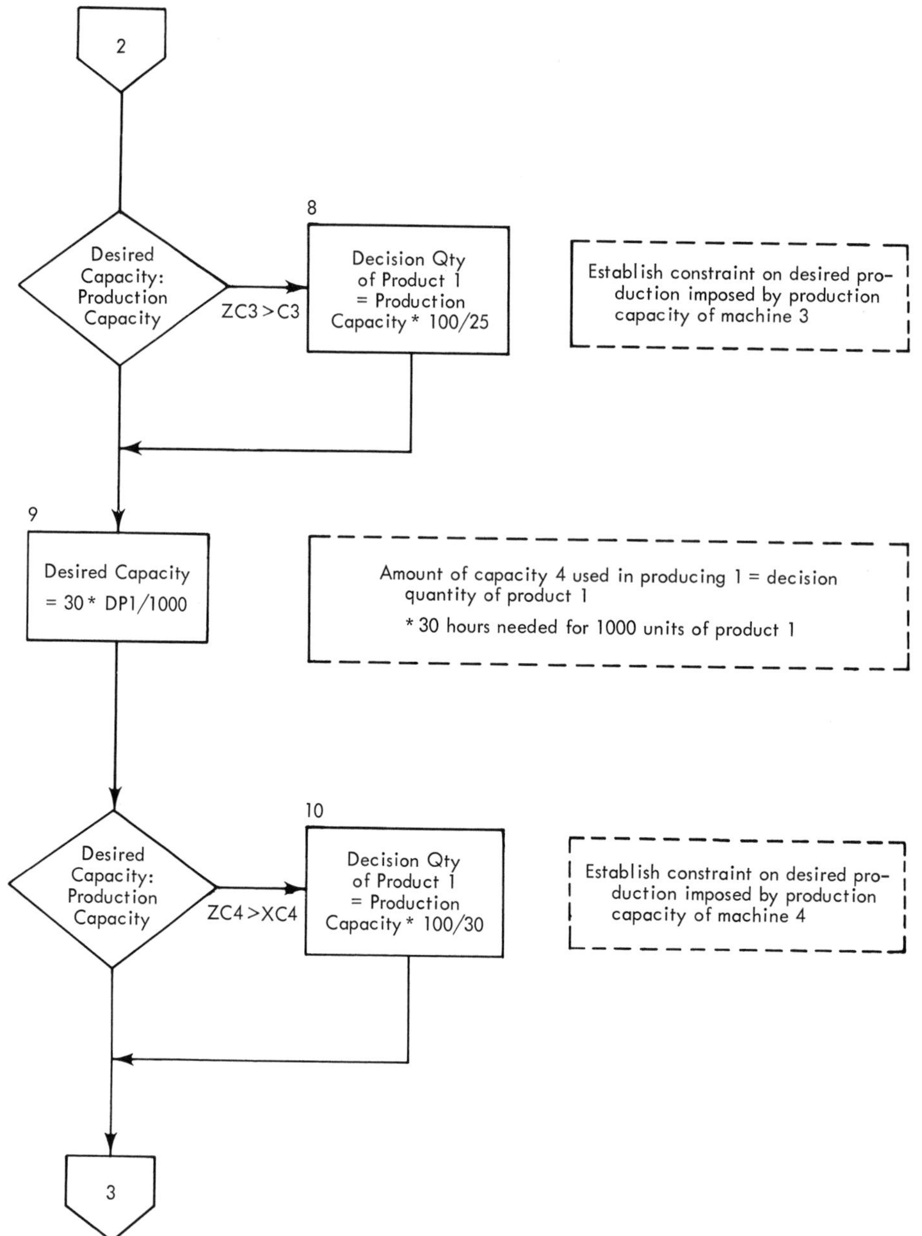
2
8
Desired Capacity: Production Capacity
ZC3 > C3
Decision Qty of Product 1 = Production Capacity * 100/25
Establish constraint on desired production imposed by production capacity of machine 3
9
Desired Capacity = 30 * DP1/1000
Amount of capacity 4 used in producing 1 = decision quantity of product 1
* 30 hours needed for 1000 units of product 1
10
Desired Capacity: Production Capacity
ZC4 > XC4
Decision Qty of Product 1 = Production Capacity * 100/30
Establish constraint on desired production imposed by production capacity of machine 4
3

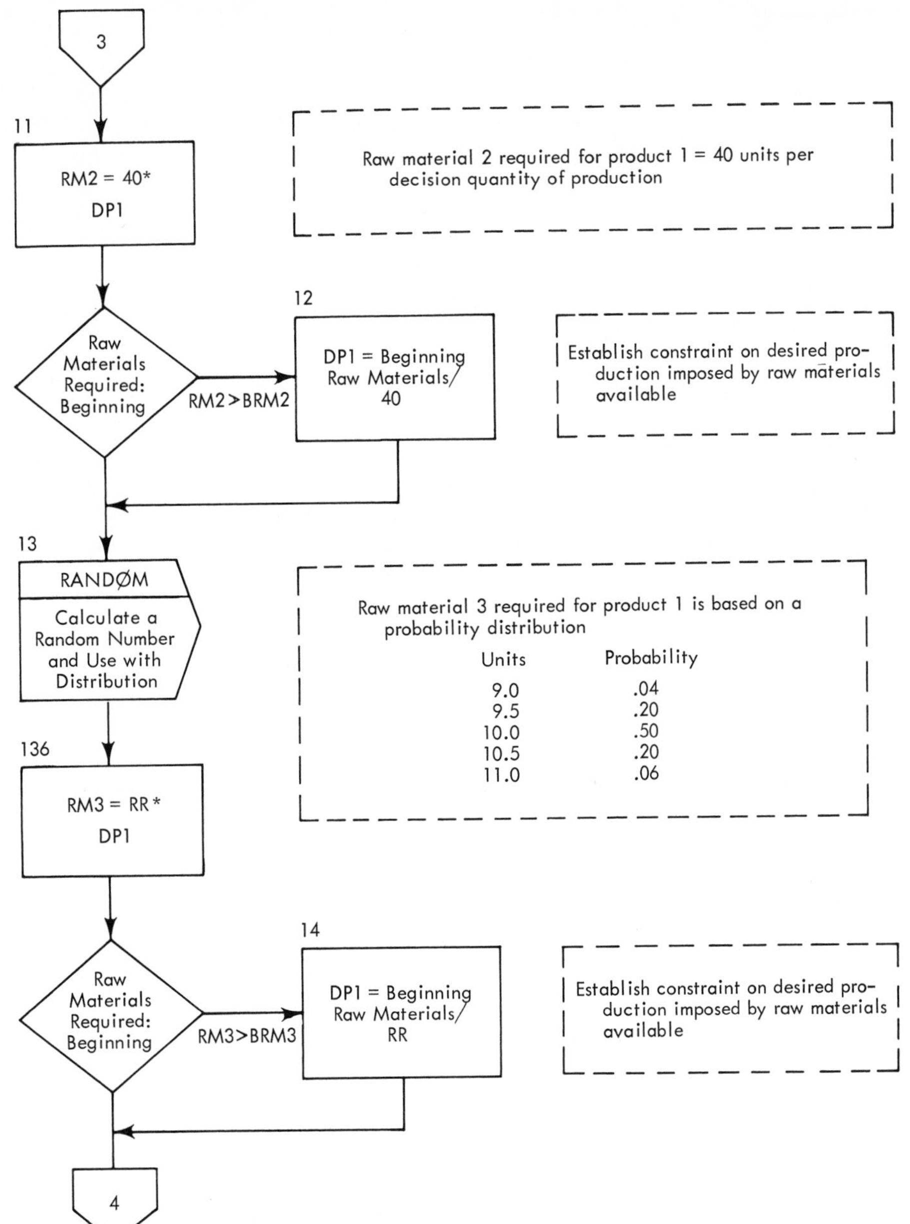

3
11
RM2 = 40*
DP1
Raw material 2 required for product 1 = 40 units per decision quantity of production
Raw Materials Required: Beginning
RM2>BRM2
12
DP1 = Beginning Raw Materials/ 40
Establish constraint on desired production imposed by raw materials available
13
RANDØM
Calculate a Random Number and Use with Distribution
Raw material 3 required for product 1 is based on a probability distribution
Units
Probability
9.0
.04
9.5
.20
10.0
.50
10.5
.20
11.0
.06
136
RM3 = RR*
DP1
14
Raw Materials Required: Beginning
RM3>BRM3
DP1 = Beginning Raw Materials/ RR
Establish constraint on desired production imposed by raw materials available
4

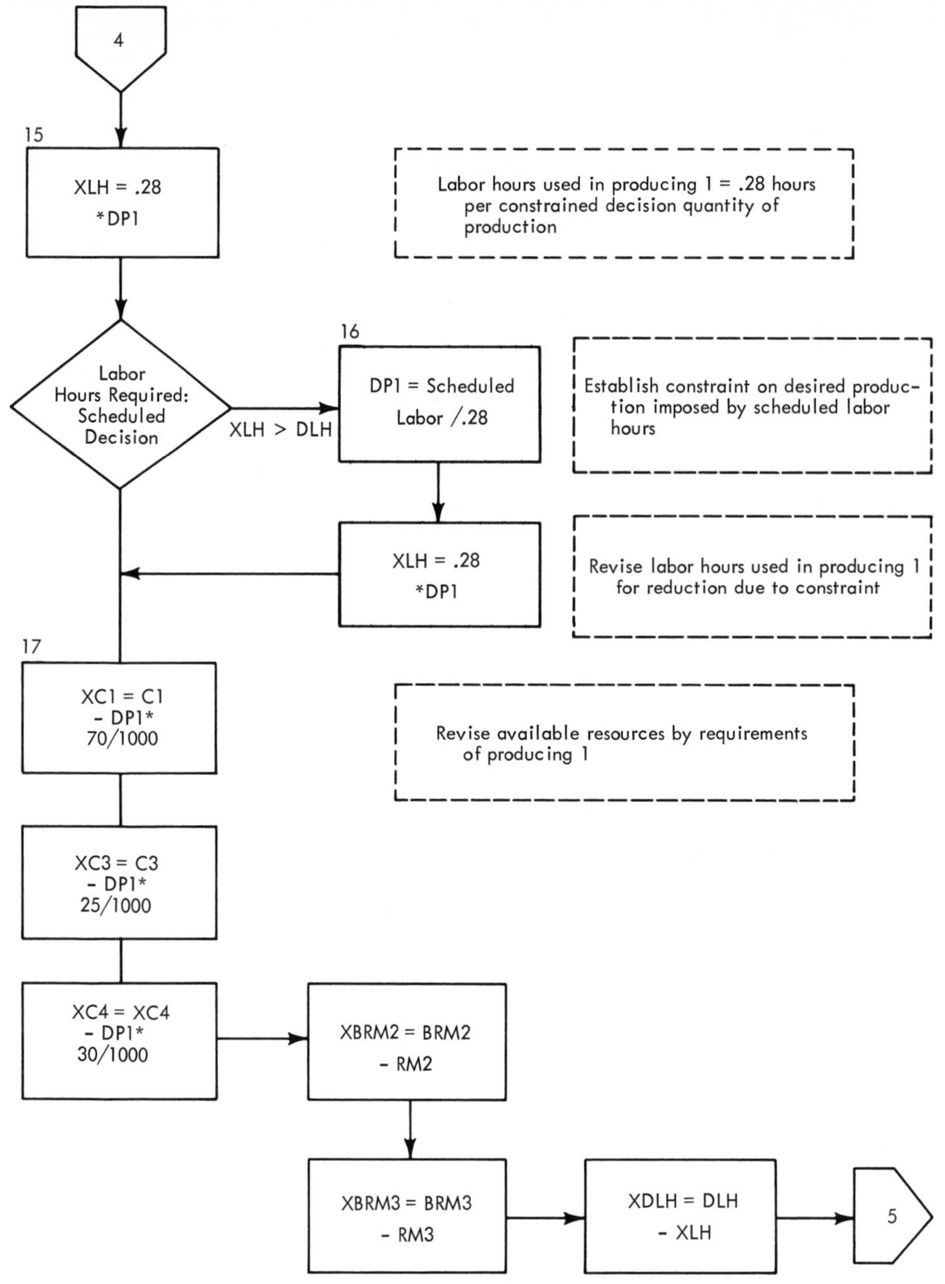
4
15
XLH = .28 *DP1
Labor hours used in producing 1 = .28 hours per constrained decision quantity of production
Labor Hours Required: Scheduled Decision
XLH > DLH
16
DP1 = Scheduled Labor /.28
Establish constraint on desired production imposed by scheduled labor hours
XLH = .28 *DP1
Revise labor hours used in producing 1 for reduction due to constraint
17
XC1 = C1 - DP1* 70/1000
Revise available resources by requirements of producing 1
XC3 = C3 - DP1* 25/1000
XC4 = XC4 - DP1* 30/1000
XBRM2 = BRM2 - RM2
XBRM3 = BRM3 - RM3
XDLH = DLH - XLH
5

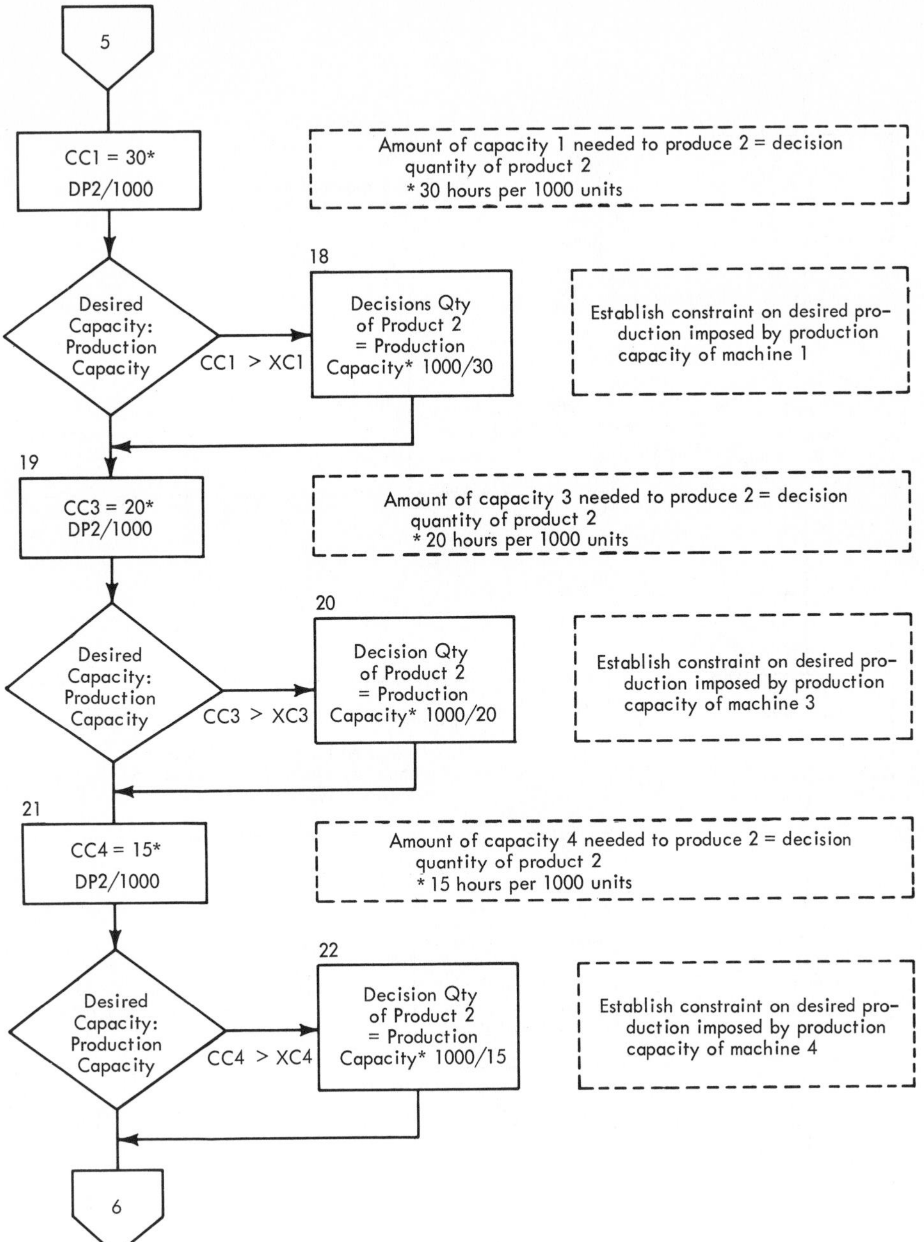
5
CC1 = 30*
DP2/1000
Amount of capacity 1 needed to produce 2 = decision quantity of product 2
* 30 hours per 1000 units
18
Desired Capacity: Production Capacity
CC1 > XC1
Decisions Qty of Product 2 = Production Capacity* 1000/30
Establish constraint on desired production imposed by production capacity of machine 1
19
CC3 = 20*
DP2/1000
Amount of capacity 3 needed to produce 2 = decision quantity of product 2
* 20 hours per 1000 units
20
Desired Capacity: Production Capacity
CC3 > XC3
Decision Qty of Product 2 = Production Capacity* 1000/20
Establish constraint on desired production imposed by production capacity of machine 3
21
CC4 = 15*
DP2/1000
Amount of capacity 4 needed to produce 2 = decision quantity of product 2
* 15 hours per 1000 units
22
Desired Capacity: Production Capacity
CC4 > XC4
Decision Qty of Product 2 = Production Capacity* 1000/15
Establish constraint on desired production imposed by production capacity of machine 4
6

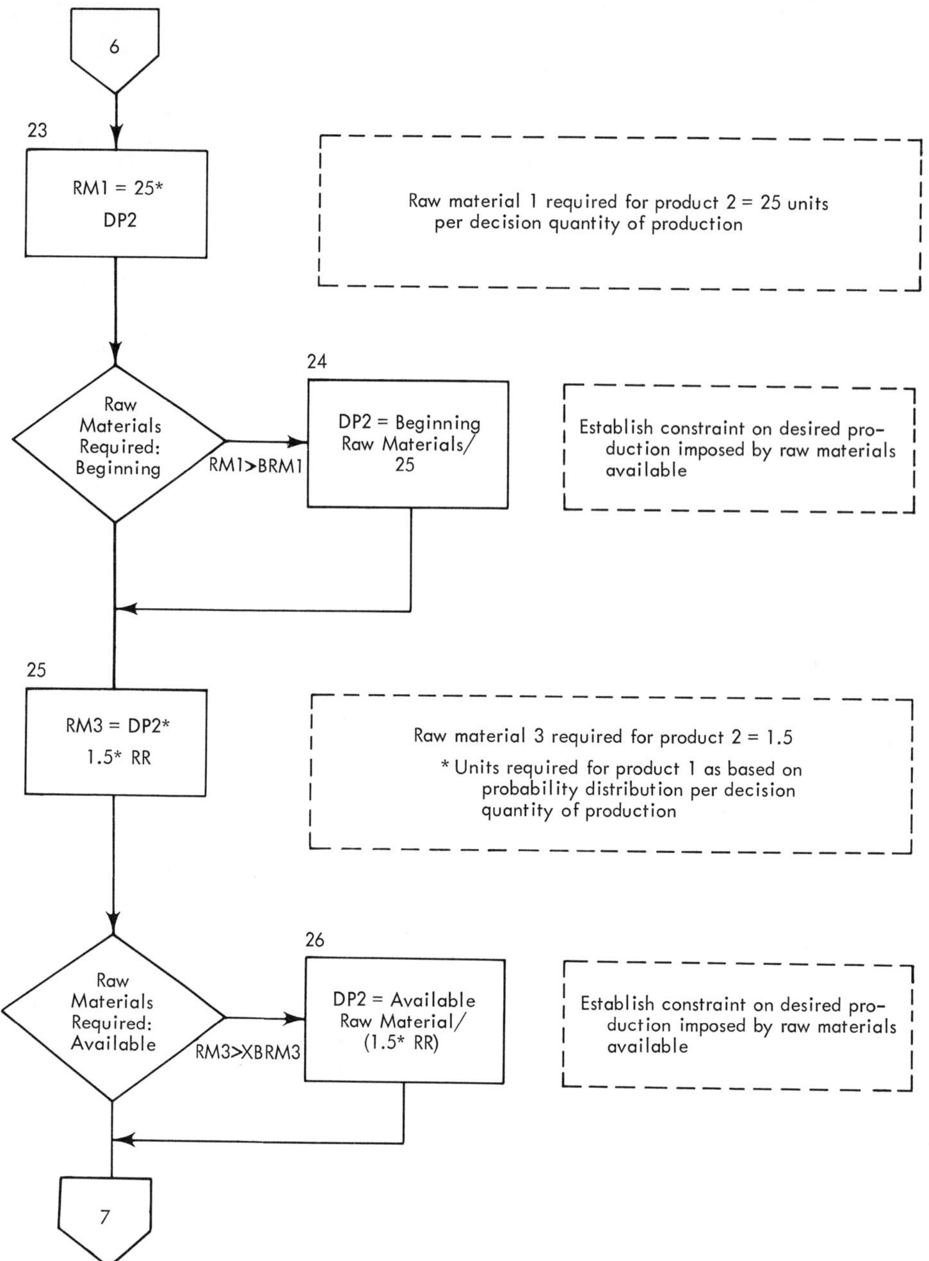
6
23
RM1 = 25*
DP2
Raw material 1 required for product 2 = 25 units per decision quantity of production
Raw Materials Required: Beginning
RM1>BRM1
24
DP2 = Beginning Raw Materials/ 25
Establish constraint on desired production imposed by raw materials available
25
RM3 = DP2* 1.5* RR
Raw material 3 required for product 2 = 1.5
* Units required for product 1 as based on probability distribution per decision quantity of production
Raw Materials Required: Available
RM3>XBRM3
26
DP2 = Available Raw Material/ (1.5* RR)
Establish constraint on desired production imposed by raw materials available
7

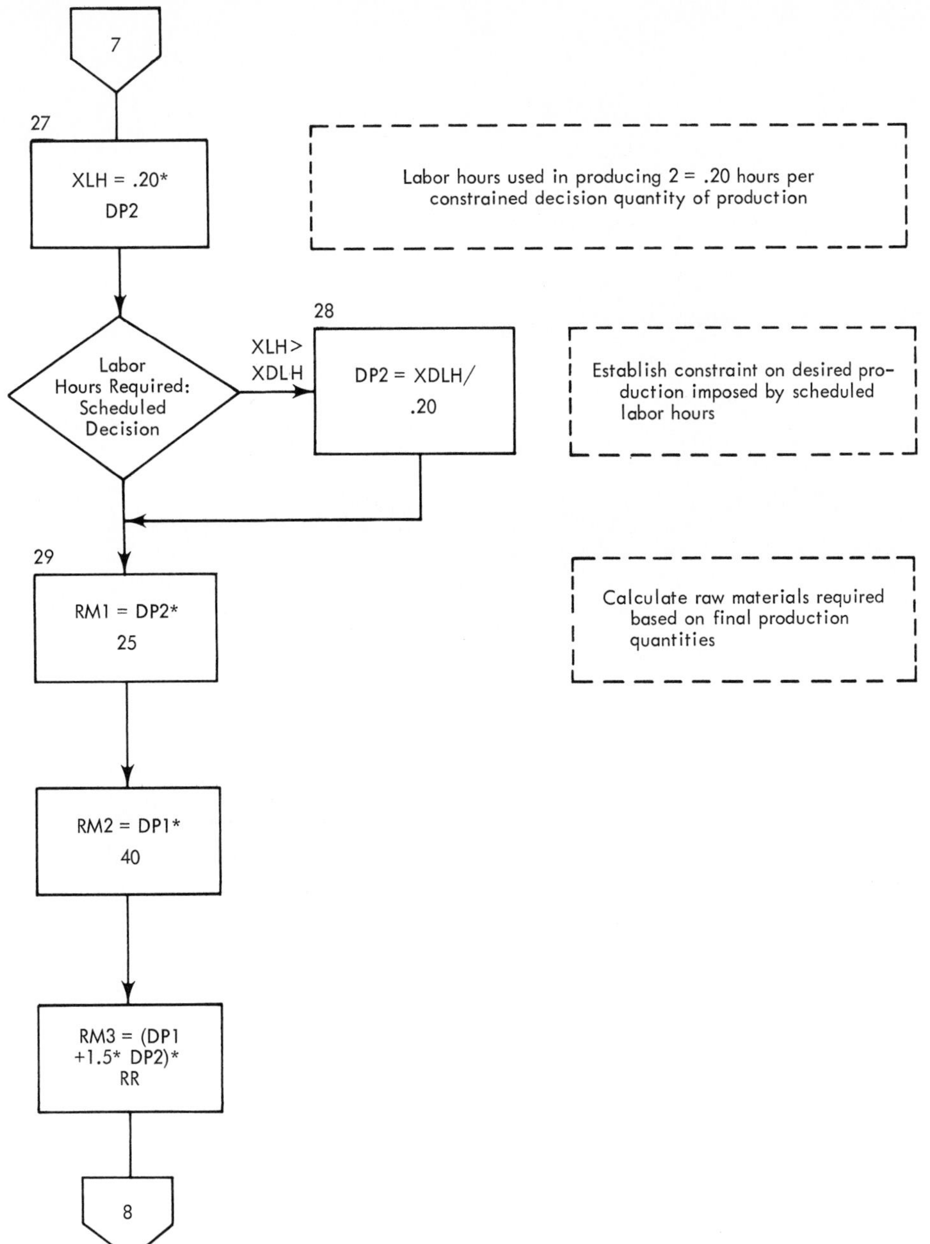
7
27
XLH = .20*
DP2
Labor hours used in producing 2 = .20 hours per
constrained decision quantity of production
28
XLH>
XDLH
Labor
Hours Required:
Scheduled
Decision
DP2 = XDLH/
.20
Establish constraint on desired pro-
duction imposed by scheduled
labor hours
29
RM1 = DP2*
25
Calculate raw materials required
based on final production
quantities
RM2 = DP1*
40
RM3 = (DP1
+1.5* DP2)*
RR
8

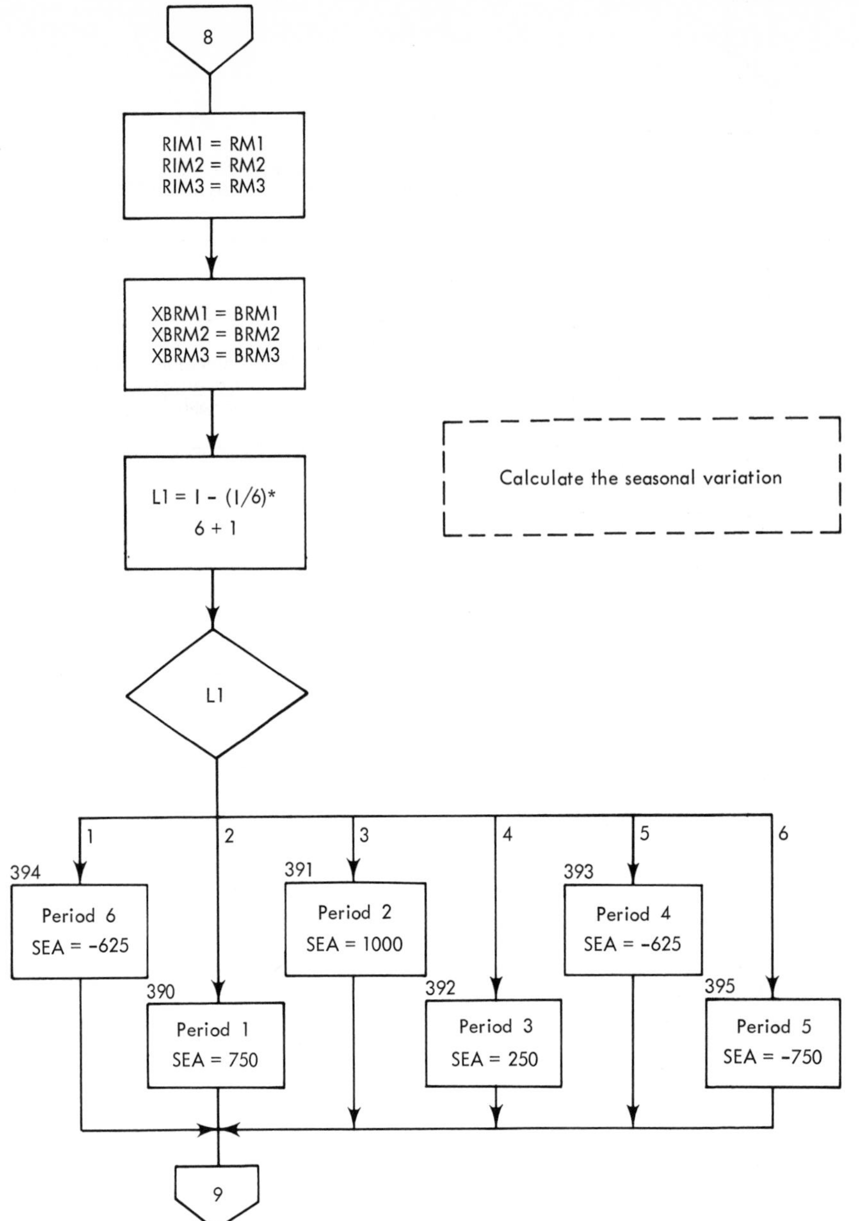
8
RIM1 = RM1
RIM2 = RM2
RIM3 = RM3
XBRM1 = BRM1
XBRM2 = BRM2
XBRM3 = BRM3
L1 = I - (I/6)*
6 + 1
Calculate the seasonal variation
L1
1
2
3
4
5
6
394
Period 6
SEA = -625
390
Period 1
SEA = 750
391
Period 2
SEA = 1000
392
Period 3
SEA = 250
393
Period 4
SEA = -625
395
Period 5
SEA = -750
9

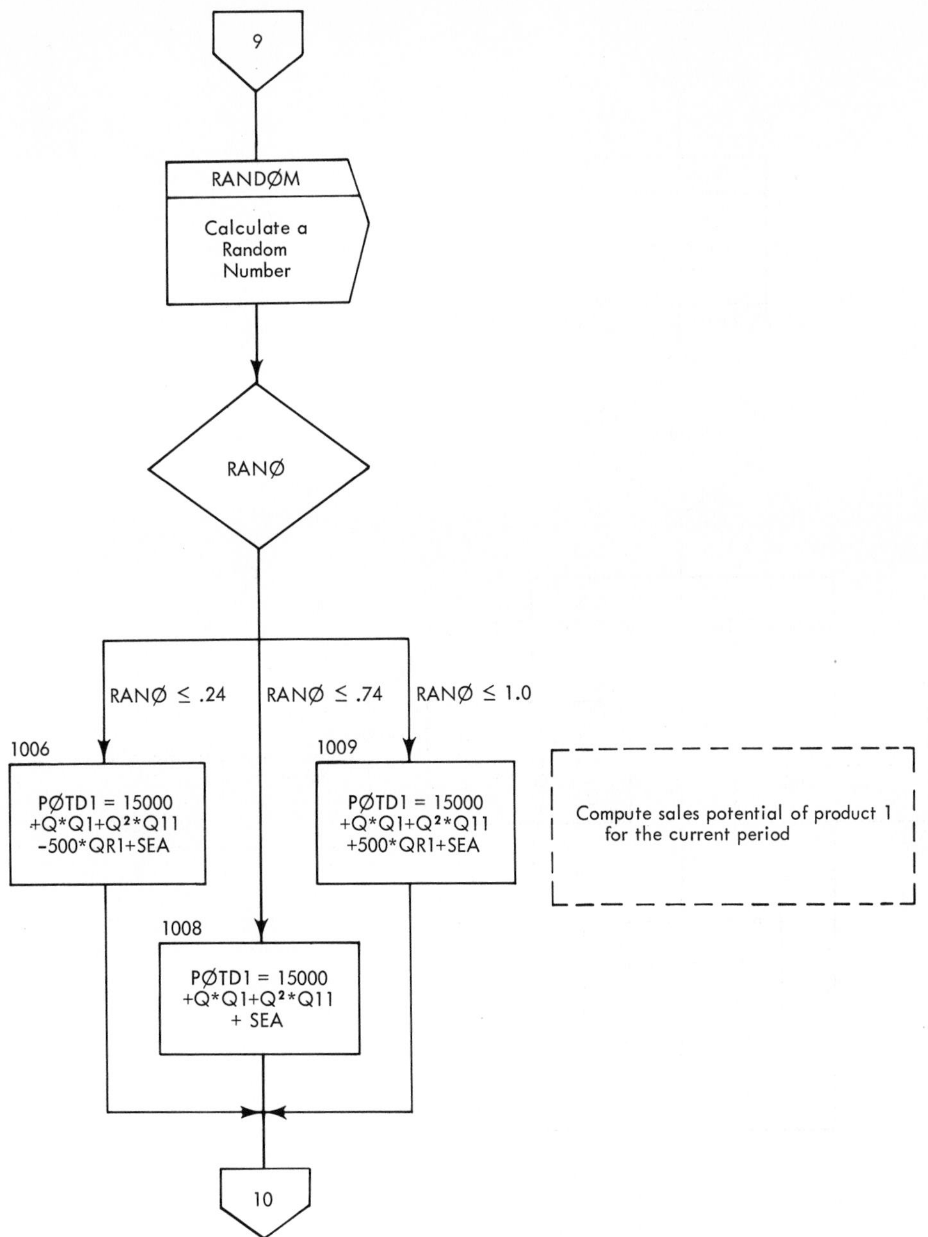

9
RANDØM
Calculate a Random Number
RANØ
RANØ ≤ .24
RANØ ≤ .74
RANØ ≤ 1.0
1006
PØTD1 = 15000 +Q*Q1+Q²*Q11 -500*QR1+SEA
1009
PØTD1 = 15000 +Q*Q1+Q²*Q11 +500*QR1+SEA
Compute sales potential of product 1 for the current period
1008
PØTD1 = 15000 +Q*Q1+Q²*Q11 + SEA
10

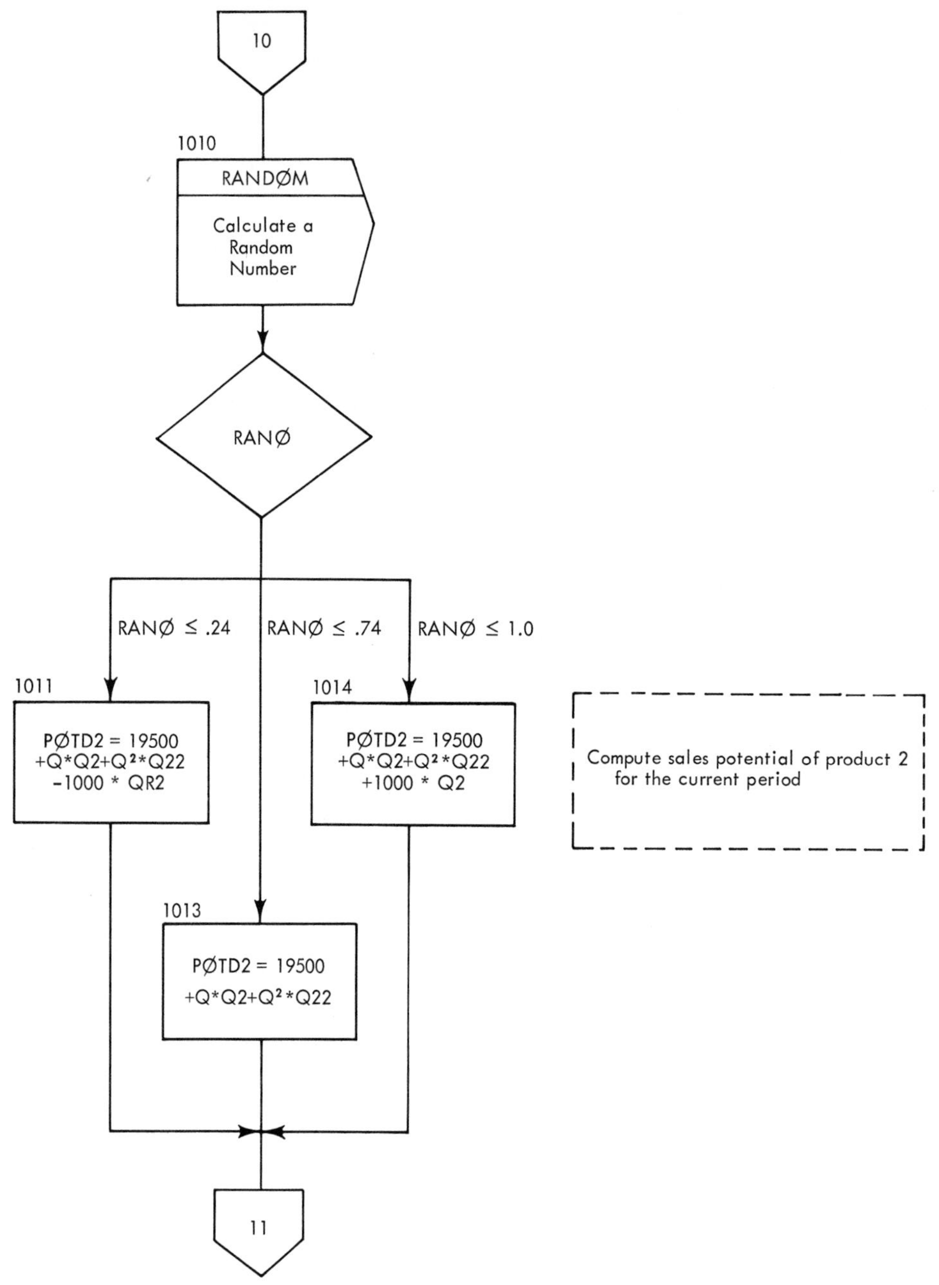
10
1010
RANDØM
Calculate a Random Number
RANØ
RANØ ≤ .24
RANØ ≤ .74
RANØ ≤ 1.0
1011
PØTD2 = 19500 +Q*Q2+Q²*Q22 -1000 * QR2
1014
PØTD2 = 19500 +Q*Q2+Q²*Q22 +1000 * Q2
Compute sales potential of product 2 for the current period
1013
PØTD2 = 19500 +Q*Q2+Q²*Q22
11

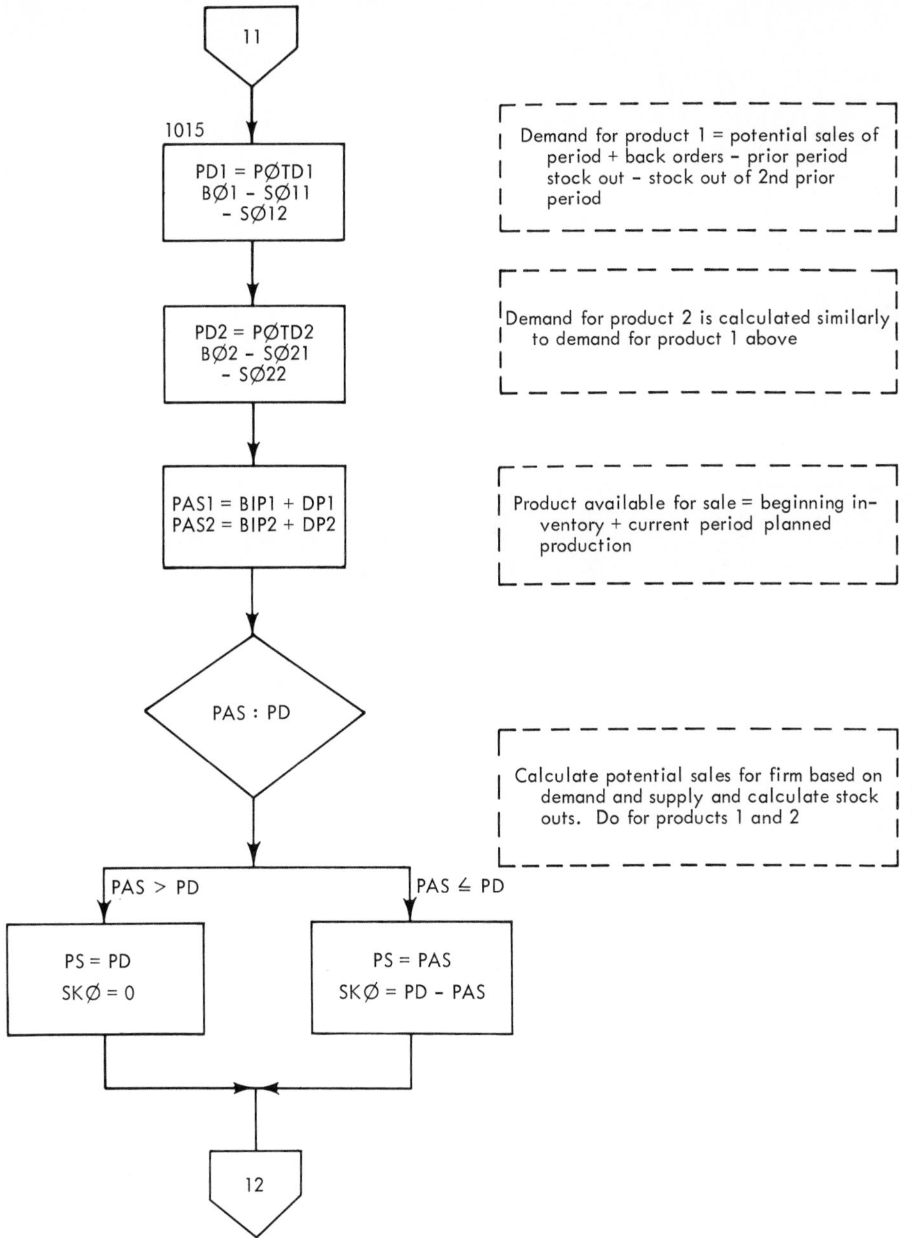
11
1015
PD1 = PØTD1
BØ1 - SØ11
- SØ12
Demand for product 1 = potential sales of period + back orders - prior period stock out - stock out of 2nd prior period
PD2 = PØTD2
BØ2 - SØ21
- SØ22
Demand for product 2 is calculated similarly to demand for product 1 above
PAS1 = BIP1 + DP1
PAS2 = BIP2 + DP2
Product available for sale = beginning inventory + current period planned production
PAS : PD
Calculate potential sales for firm based on demand and supply and calculate stock outs. Do for products 1 and 2
PAS > PD
PAS ≦ PD
PS = PD
SKØ = 0
PS = PAS
SKØ = PD - PAS
12

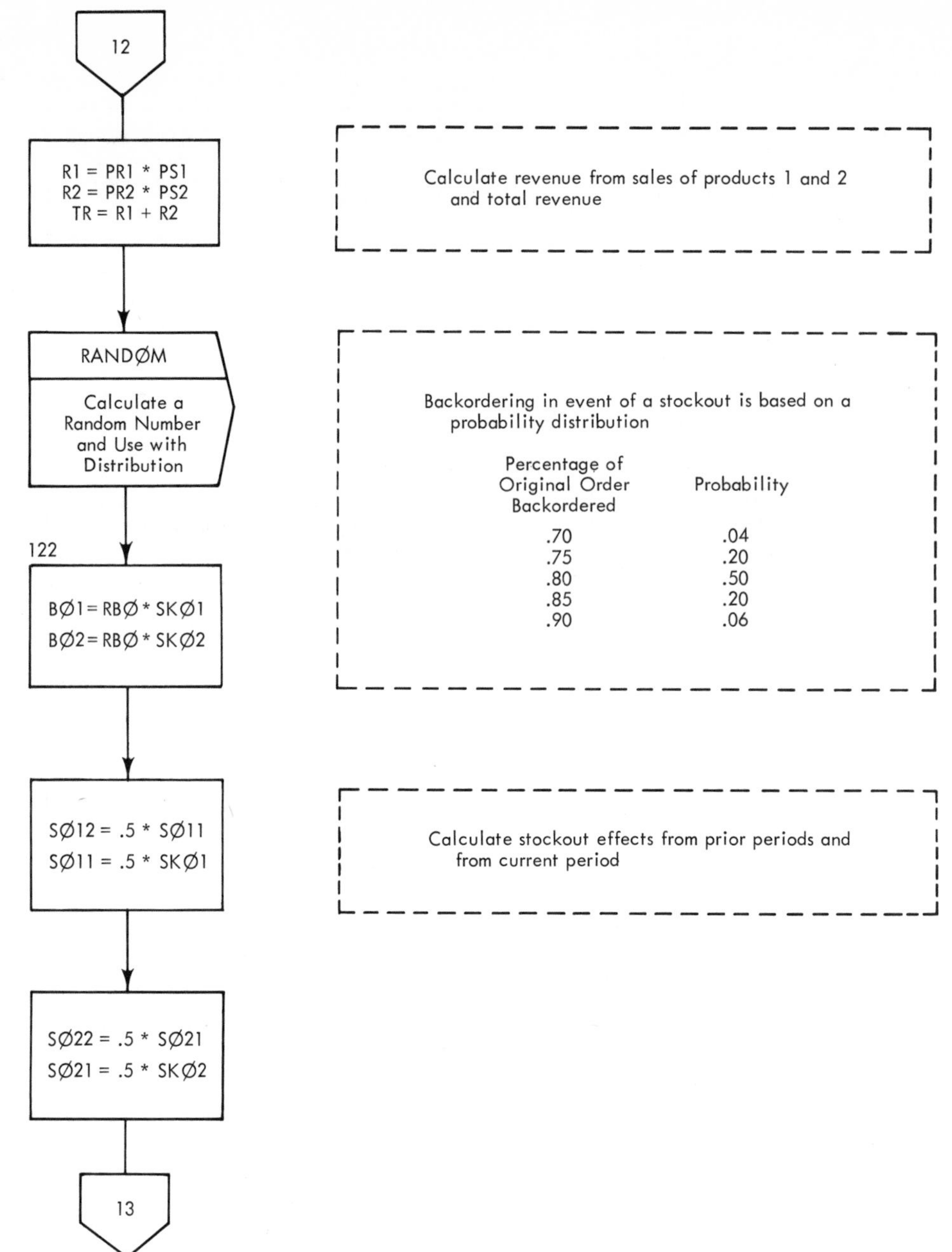

12
R1 = PR1 * PS1
R2 = PR2 * PS2
TR = R1 + R2
Calculate revenue from sales of products 1 and 2 and total revenue
RANDØM
Calculate a Random Number and Use with Distribution
Backordering in event of a stockout is based on a probability distribution
Percentage of Original Order Backordered
Probability
.70 .04
.75 .20
.80 .50
.85 .20
.90 .06
122
BØ1= RBØ * SKØ1
BØ2= RBØ * SKØ2
SØ12 = .5 * SØ11
SØ11 = .5 * SKØ1
Calculate stockout effects from prior periods and from current period
SØ22 = .5 * SØ21
SØ21 = .5 * SKØ2
13

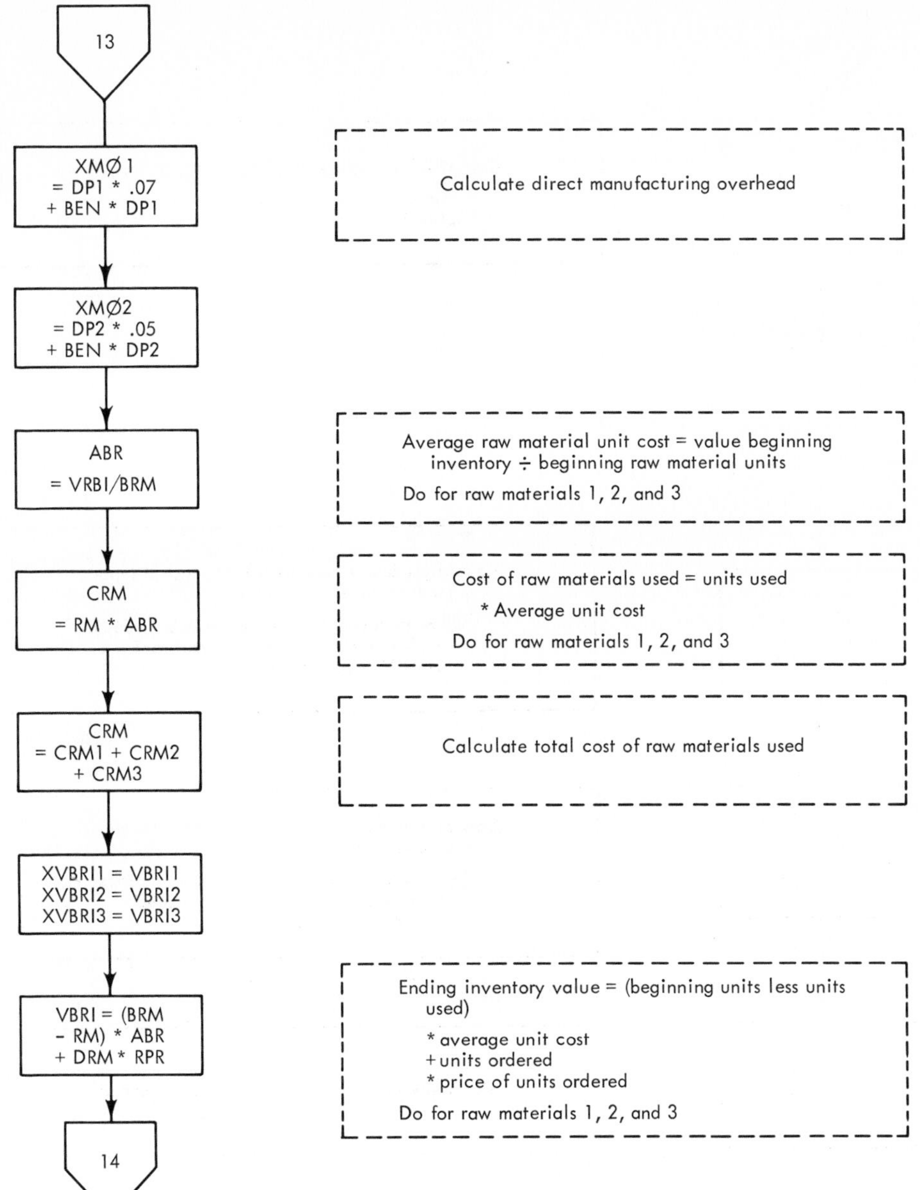
13
XMØ1
= DP1 * .07
+ BEN * DP1
Calculate direct manufacturing overhead
XMØ2
= DP2 * .05
+ BEN * DP2
ABR
= VRBI/BRM
Average raw material unit cost = value beginning inventory ÷ beginning raw material units
Do for raw materials 1, 2, and 3
CRM
= RM * ABR
Cost of raw materials used = units used
* Average unit cost
Do for raw materials 1, 2, and 3
CRM
= CRM1 + CRM2
+ CRM3
Calculate total cost of raw materials used
XVBRI1 = VBRI1
XVBRI2 = VBRI2
XVBRI3 = VBRI3
VBRI = (BRM
- RM) * ABR
+ DRM * RPR
Ending inventory value = (beginning units less units used)
* average unit cost
+ units ordered
* price of units ordered
Do for raw materials 1, 2, and 3
14

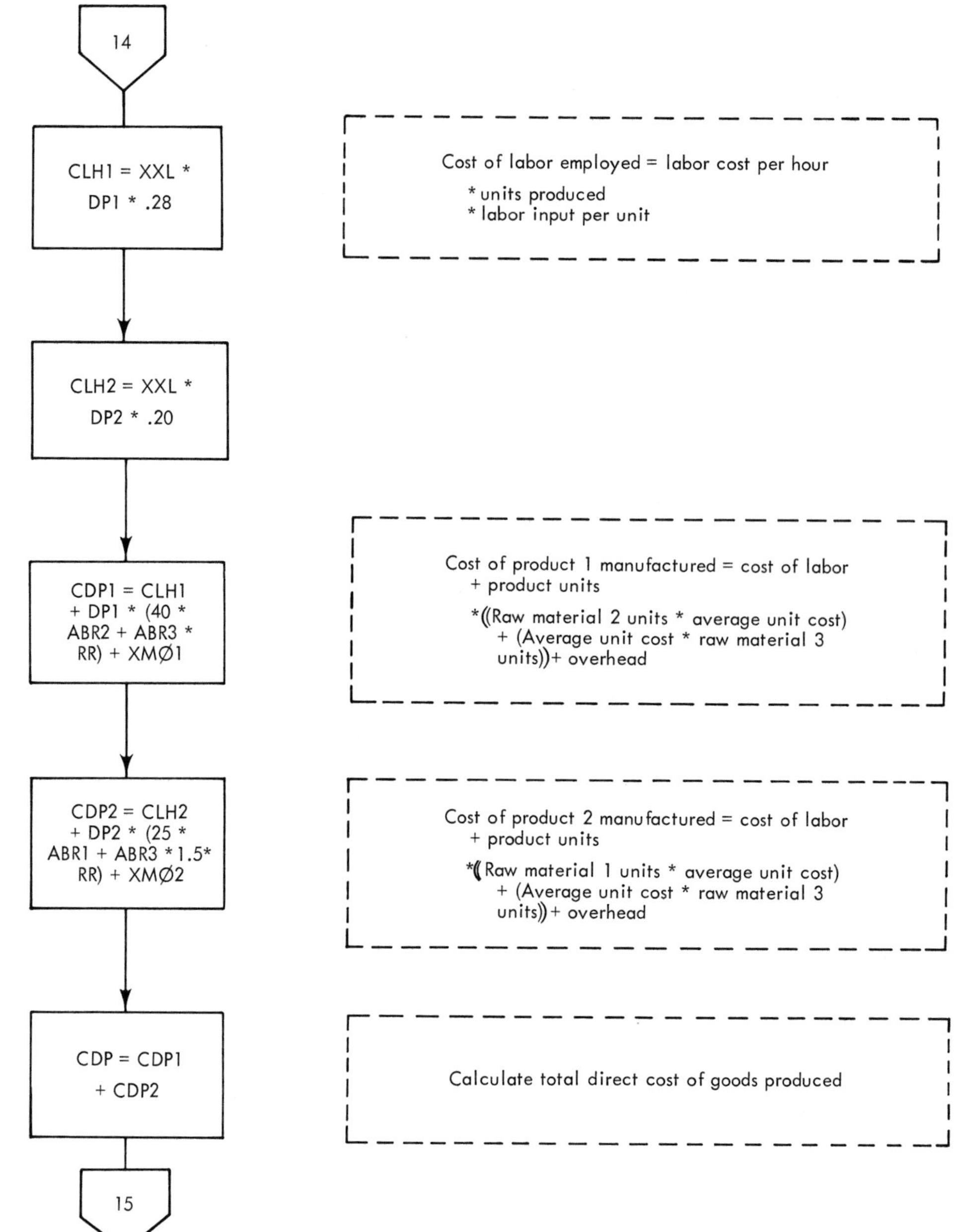
14
CLH1 = XXL * DP1 * .28
Cost of labor employed = labor cost per hour * units produced * labor input per unit
CLH2 = XXL * DP2 * .20
CDP1 = CLH1 + DP1 * (40 * ABR2 + ABR3 * RR) + XMØ1
Cost of product 1 manufactured = cost of labor + product units *((Raw material 2 units * average unit cost) + (Average unit cost * raw material 3 units))+ overhead
CDP2 = CLH2 + DP2 * (25 * ABR1 + ABR3 * 1.5* RR) + XMØ2
Cost of product 2 manufactured = cost of labor + product units *((Raw material 1 units * average unit cost) + (Average unit cost * raw material 3 units))+ overhead
CDP = CDP1 + CDP2
Calculate total direct cost of goods produced
15

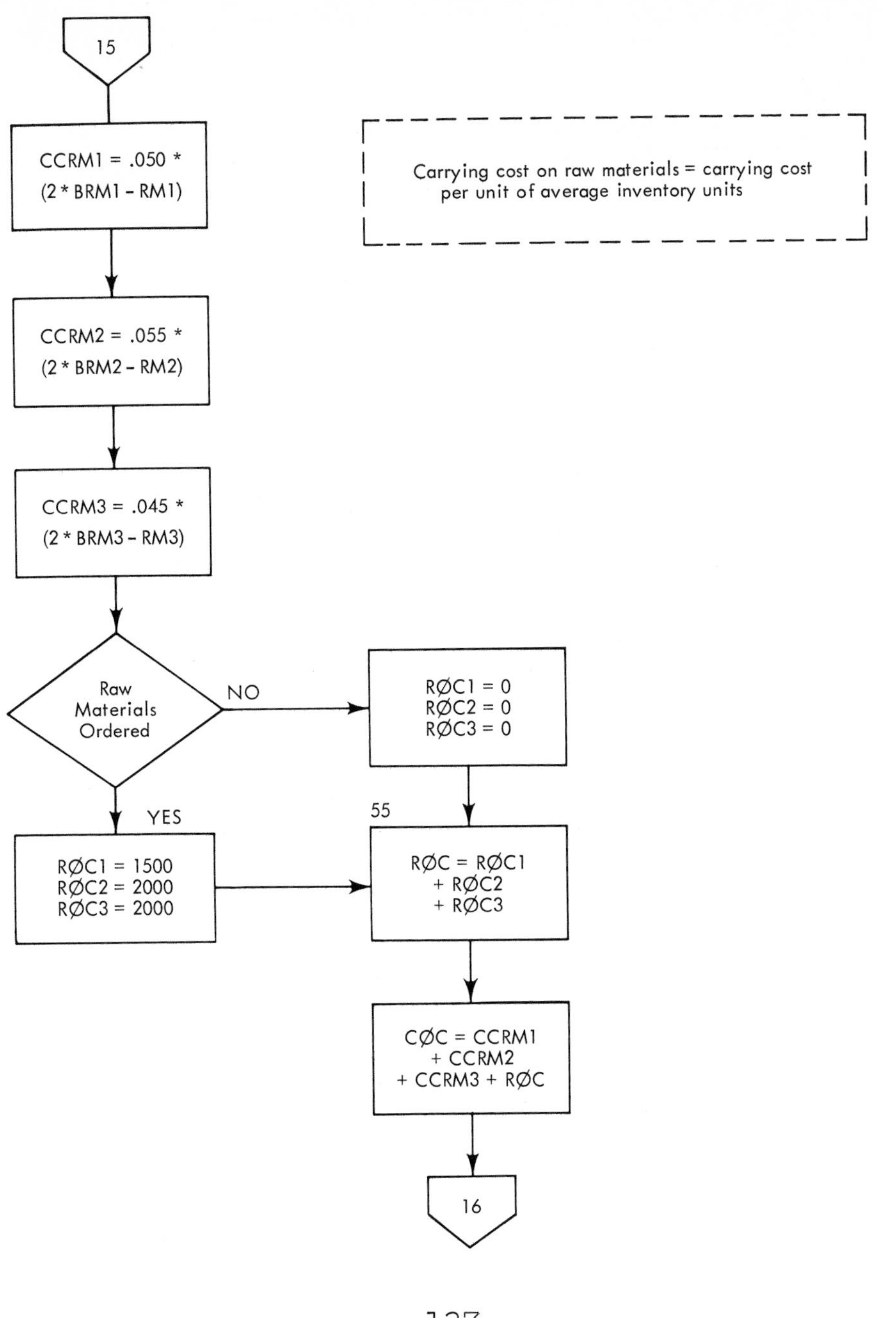
15
CCRM1 = .050 *
(2 * BRM1 - RM1)
Carrying cost on raw materials = carrying cost
per unit of average inventory units
CCRM2 = .055 *
(2 * BRM2 - RM2)
CCRM3 = .045 *
(2 * BRM3 - RM3)
Raw
Materials
Ordered
NO
RØC1 = 0
RØC2 = 0
RØC3 = 0
YES
55
RØC1 = 1500
RØC2 = 2000
RØC3 = 2000
RØC = RØC1
+ RØC2
+ RØC3
CØC = CCRM1
+ CCRM2
+ CCRM3 + RØC
16

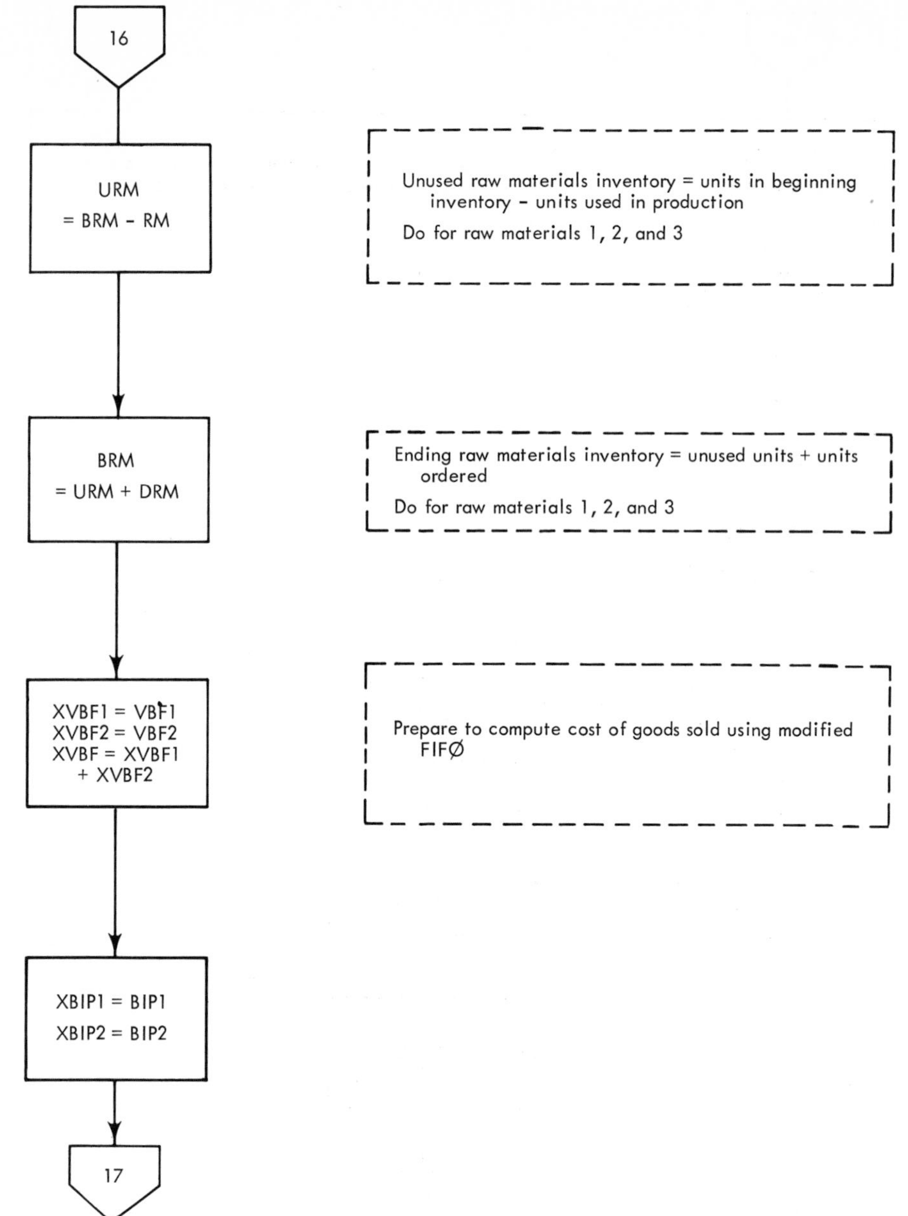

16
URM
= BRM - RM
Unused raw materials inventory = units in beginning inventory - units used in production
Do for raw materials 1, 2, and 3
BRM
= URM + DRM
Ending raw materials inventory = unused units + units ordered
Do for raw materials 1, 2, and 3
XVBF1 = VBF1
XVBF2 = VBF2
XVBF = XVBF1
+ XVBF2
Prepare to compute cost of goods sold using modified FIFØ
XBIP1 = BIP1
XBIP2 = BIP2
17

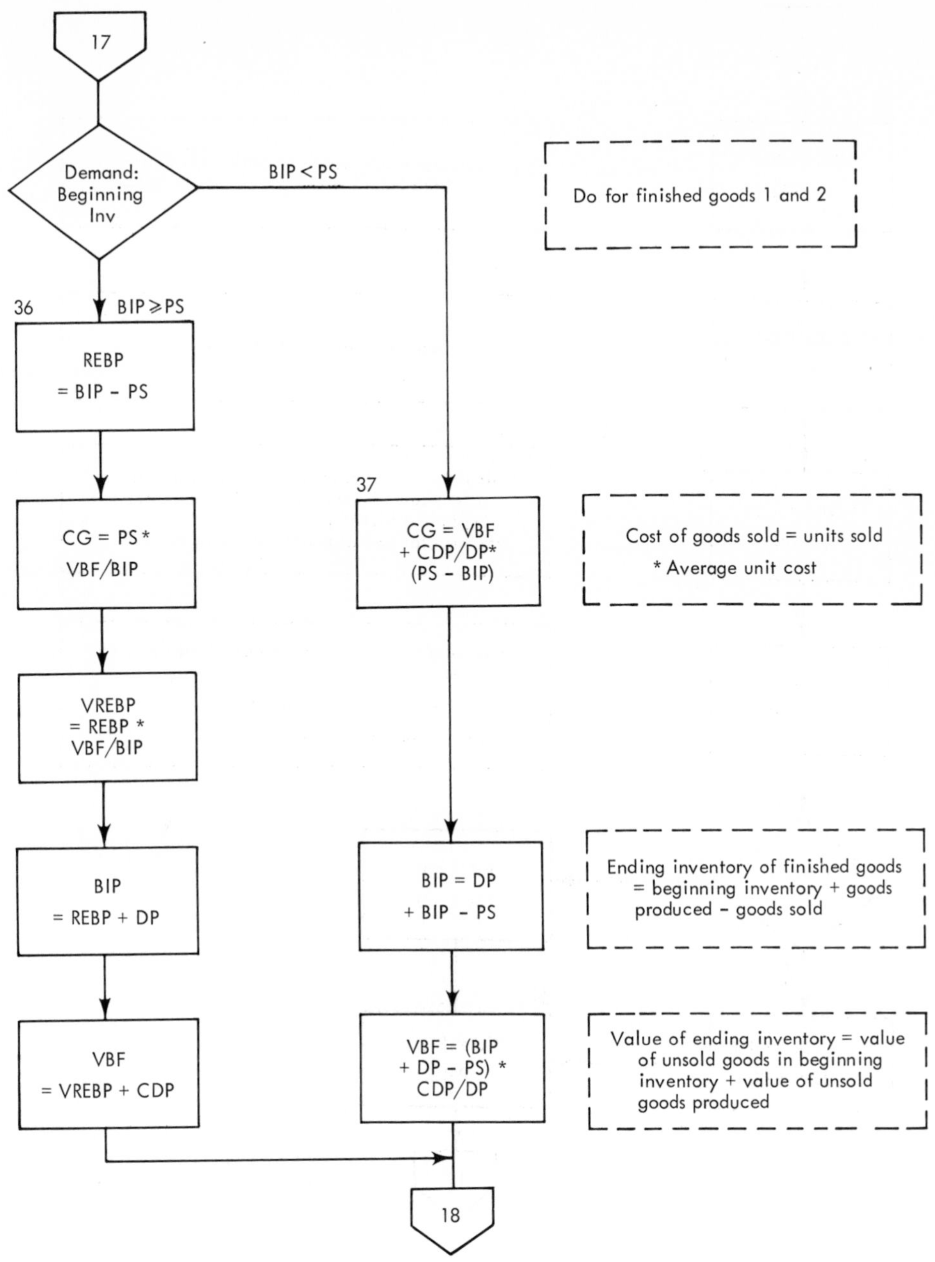
17
Demand: Beginning Inv
BIP < PS
Do for finished goods 1 and 2
36
BIP ≥ PS
REBP = BIP - PS
37
CG = PS * VBF/BIP
CG = VBF + CDP/DP* (PS - BIP)
Cost of goods sold = units sold * Average unit cost
VREBP = REBP * VBF/BIP
BIP = REBP + DP
BIP = DP + BIP - PS
Ending inventory of finished goods = beginning inventory + goods produced - goods sold
VBF = VREBP + CDP
VBF = (BIP + DP - PS) * CDP/DP
Value of ending inventory = value of unsold goods in beginning inventory + value of unsold goods produced
18

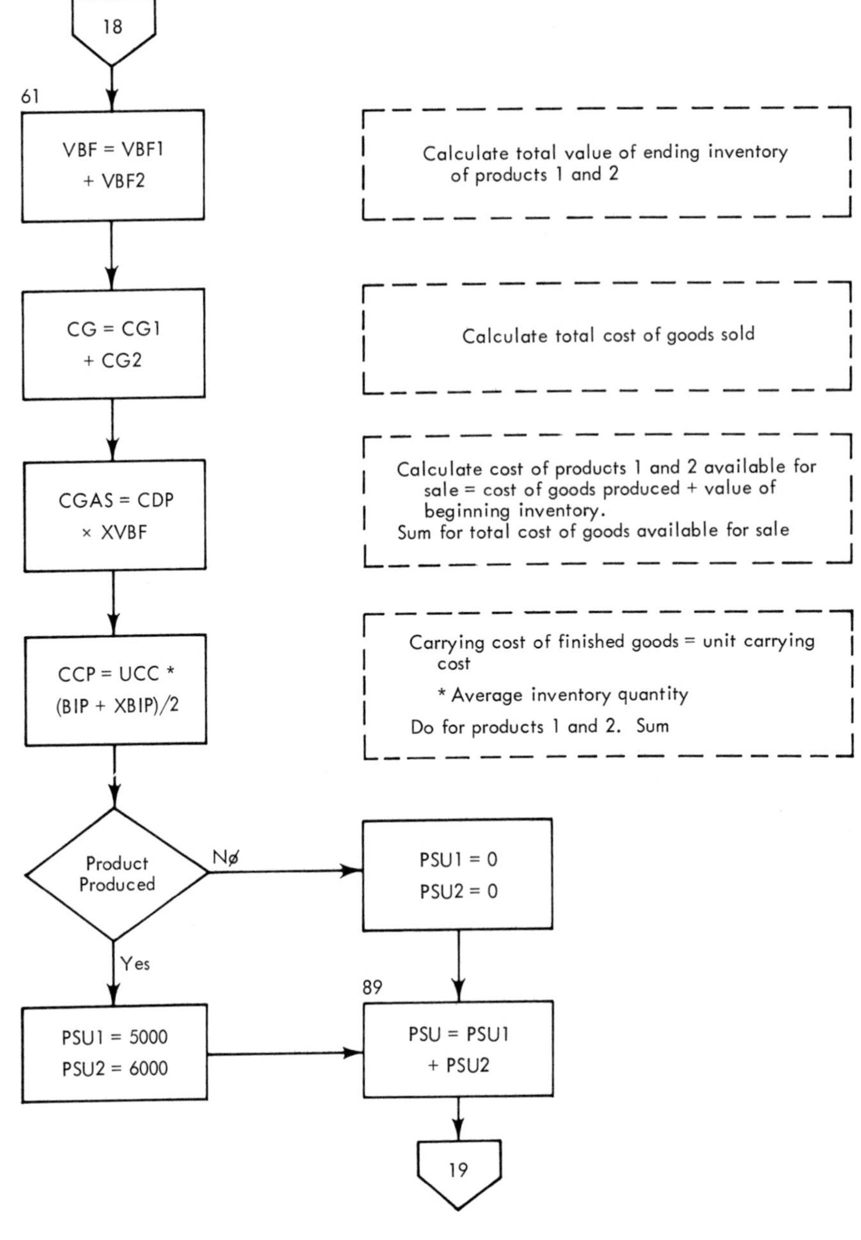

18
61
VBF = VBF1
+ VBF2
Calculate total value of ending inventory
of products 1 and 2
CG = CG1
+ CG2
Calculate total cost of goods sold
CGAS = CDP
× XVBF
Calculate cost of products 1 and 2 available for
sale = cost of goods produced + value of
beginning inventory.
Sum for total cost of goods available for sale
CCP = UCC *
(BIP + XBIP)/2
Carrying cost of finished goods = unit carrying
cost
* Average inventory quantity
Do for products 1 and 2. Sum
Product
Produced
Nø
PSU1 = 0
PSU2 = 0
Yes
89
PSU1 = 5000
PSU2 = 6000
PSU = PSU1
+ PSU2
19

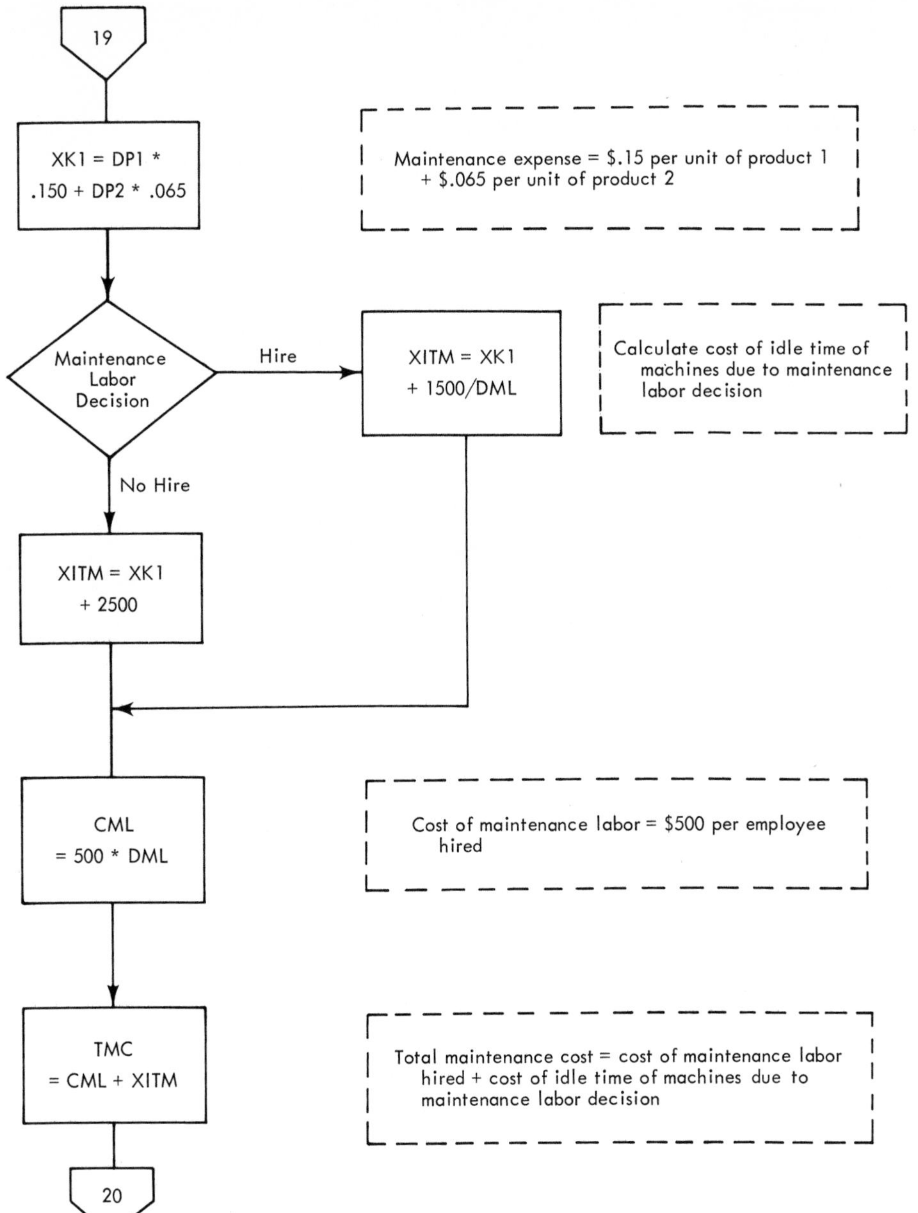
19
XK1 = DP1 *
.150 + DP2 * .065
Maintenance expense = $.15 per unit of product 1
+ $.065 per unit of product 2
Maintenance
Labor
Decision
Hire
XITM = XK1
+ 1500/DML
Calculate cost of idle time of
machines due to maintenance
labor decision
No Hire
XITM = XK1
+ 2500
CML
= 500 * DML
Cost of maintenance labor = $500 per employee
hired
TMC
= CML + XITM
Total maintenance cost = cost of maintenance labor
hired + cost of idle time of machines due to
maintenance labor decision
20

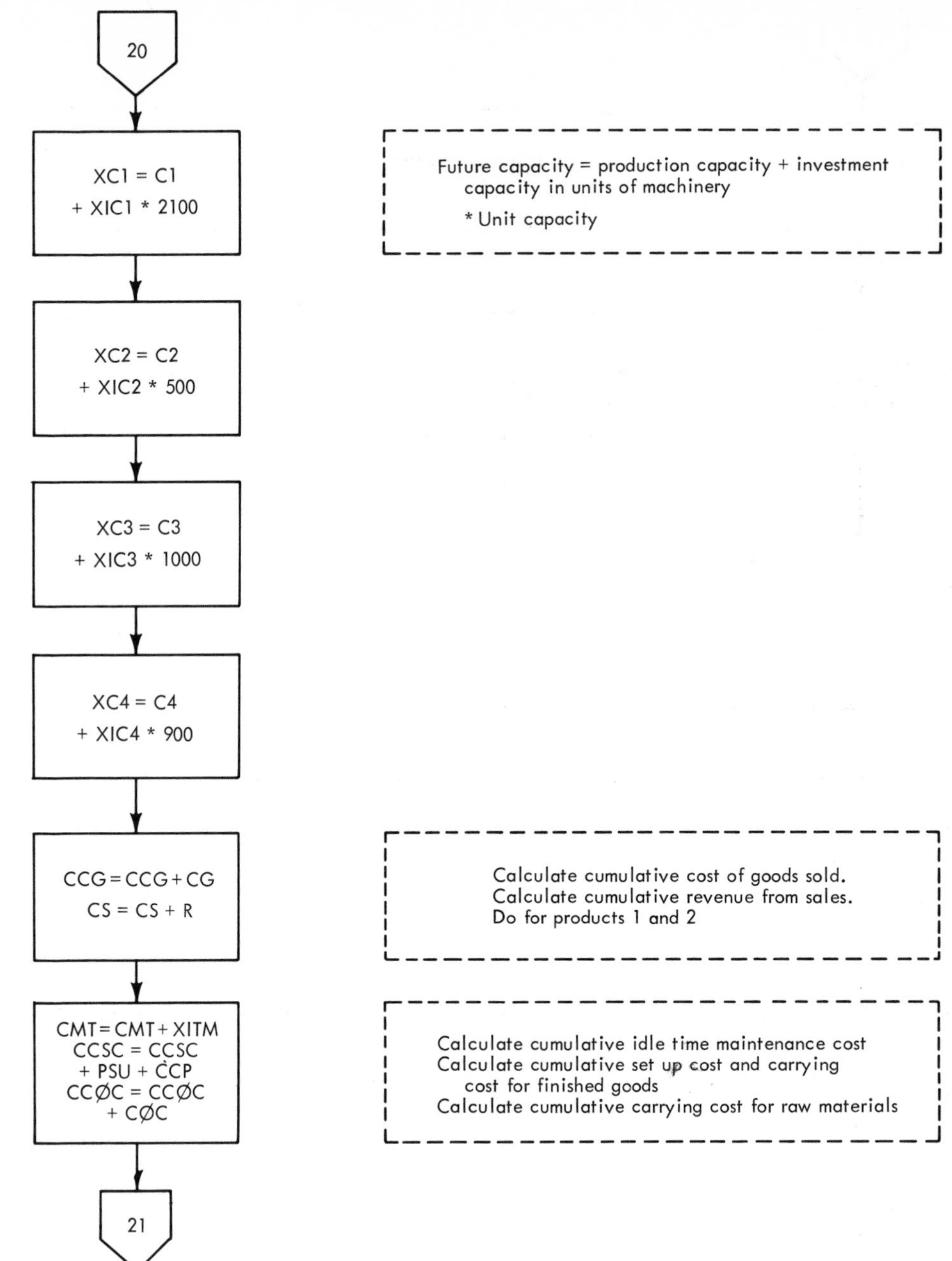

20
XC1 = C1
+ XIC1 * 2100
Future capacity = production capacity + investment capacity in units of machinery
* Unit capacity
XC2 = C2
+ XIC2 * 500
XC3 = C3
+ XIC3 * 1000
XC4 = C4
+ XIC4 * 900
CCG = CCG + CG
CS = CS + R
Calculate cumulative cost of goods sold.
Calculate cumulative revenue from sales.
Do for products 1 and 2
CMT = CMT + XITM
CCSC = CCSC
+ PSU + CCP
CCØC = CCØC
+ CØC
Calculate cumulative idle time maintenance cost
Calculate cumulative set up cost and carrying cost for finished goods
Calculate cumulative carrying cost for raw materials
21

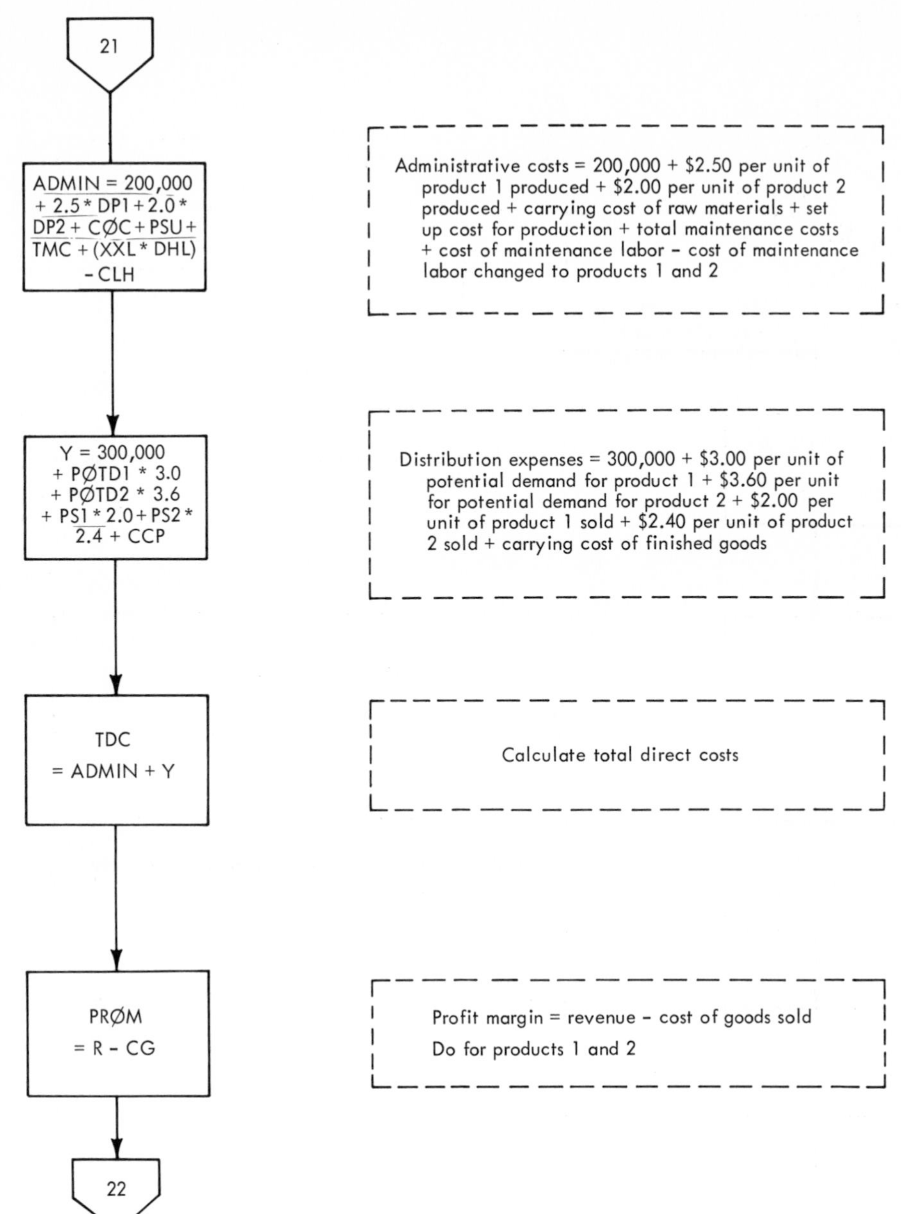
21
ADMIN = 200,000 + 2.5 * DP1 + 2.0 * DP2 + CØC + PSU + TMC + (XXL * DHL) - CLH
Administrative costs = 200,000 + $2.50 per unit of product 1 produced + $2.00 per unit of product 2 produced + carrying cost of raw materials + set up cost for production + total maintenance costs + cost of maintenance labor - cost of maintenance labor changed to products 1 and 2
Y = 300,000 + PØTD1 * 3.0 + PØTD2 * 3.6 + PS1 * 2.0 + PS2 * 2.4 + CCP
Distribution expenses = 300,000 + $3.00 per unit of potential demand for product 1 + $3.60 per unit for potential demand for product 2 + $2.00 per unit of product 1 sold + $2.40 per unit of product 2 sold + carrying cost of finished goods
TDC = ADMIN + Y
Calculate total direct costs
PRØM = R - CG
Profit margin = revenue - cost of goods sold
Do for products 1 and 2
22

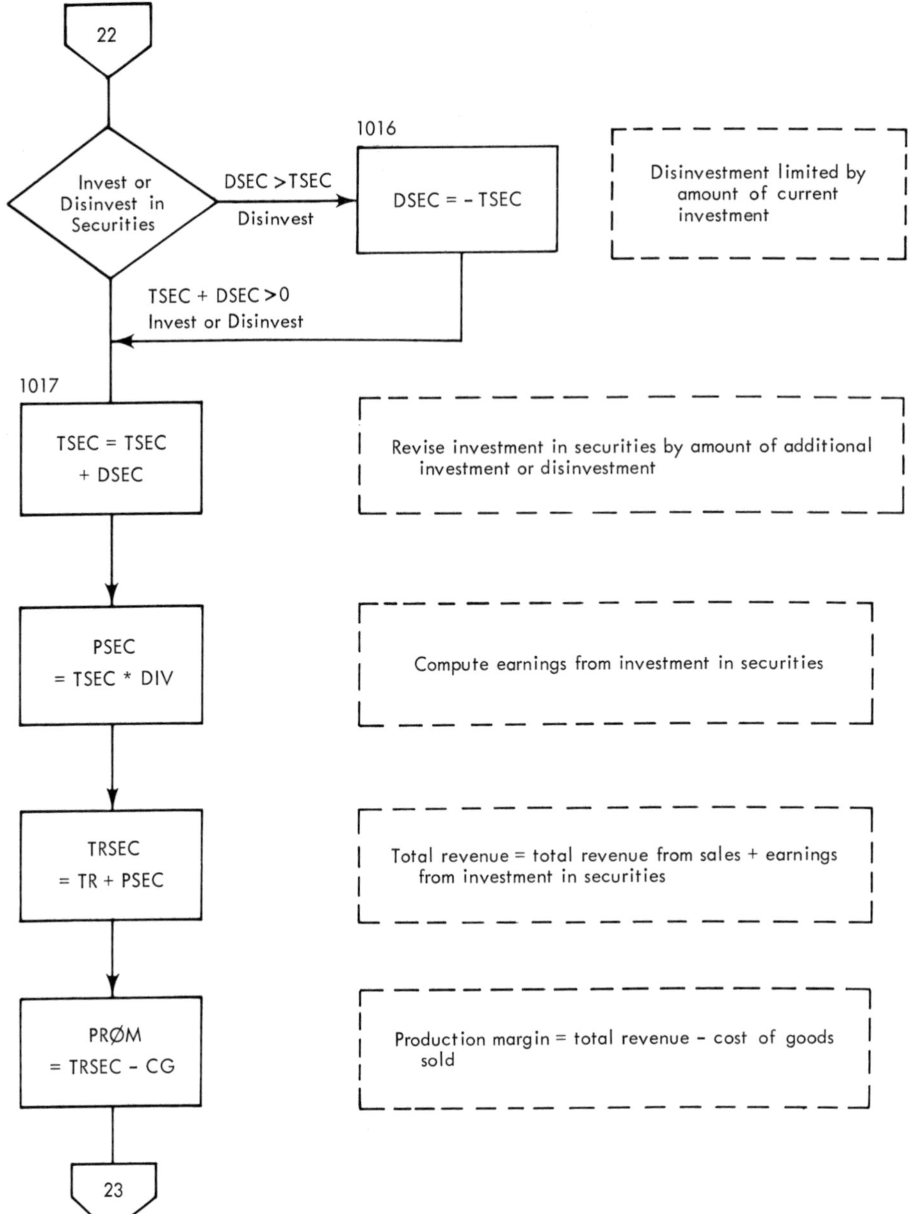
22
Invest or Disinvest in Securities
DSEC >TSEC
Disinvest
1016
DSEC = - TSEC
Disinvestment limited by amount of current investment
TSEC + DSEC >0
Invest or Disinvest
1017
TSEC = TSEC + DSEC
Revise investment in securities by amount of additional investment or disinvestment
PSEC = TSEC * DIV
Compute earnings from investment in securities
TRSEC = TR + PSEC
Total revenue = total revenue from sales + earnings from investment in securities
PRØM = TRSEC - CG
Production margin = total revenue - cost of goods sold
23

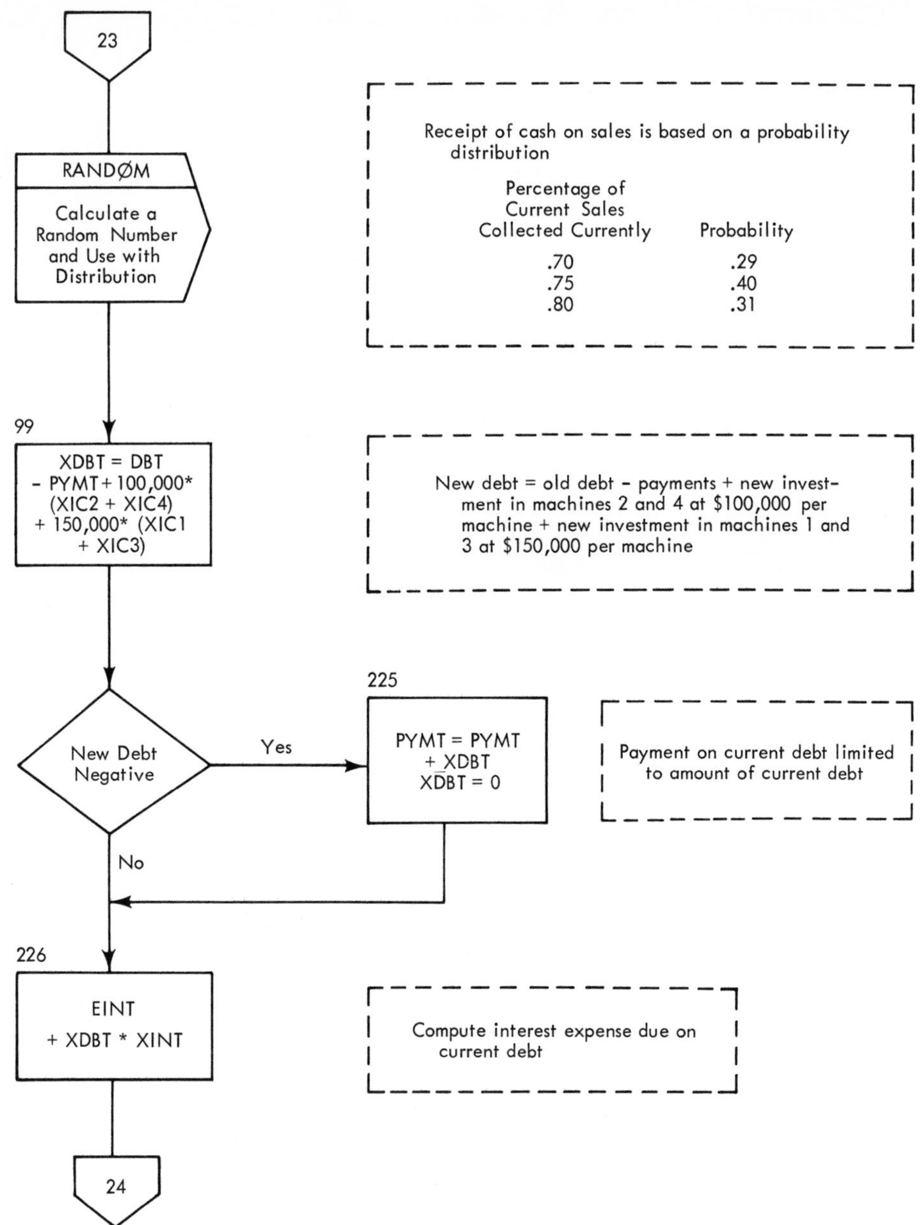
23
RANDØM
Calculate a Random Number and Use with Distribution
Receipt of cash on sales is based on a probability distribution
Percentage of Current Sales Collected Currently
Probability
.70
.29
.75
.40
.80
.31
99
XDBT = DBT - PYMT + 100,000* (XIC2 + XIC4) + 150,000* (XIC1 + XIC3)
New debt = old debt - payments + new investment in machines 2 and 4 at $100,000 per machine + new investment in machines 1 and 3 at $150,000 per machine
New Debt Negative
Yes
225
PYMT = PYMT + XDBT
XDBT = 0
Payment on current debt limited to amount of current debt
No
226
EINT + XDBT * XINT
Compute interest expense due on current debt
24

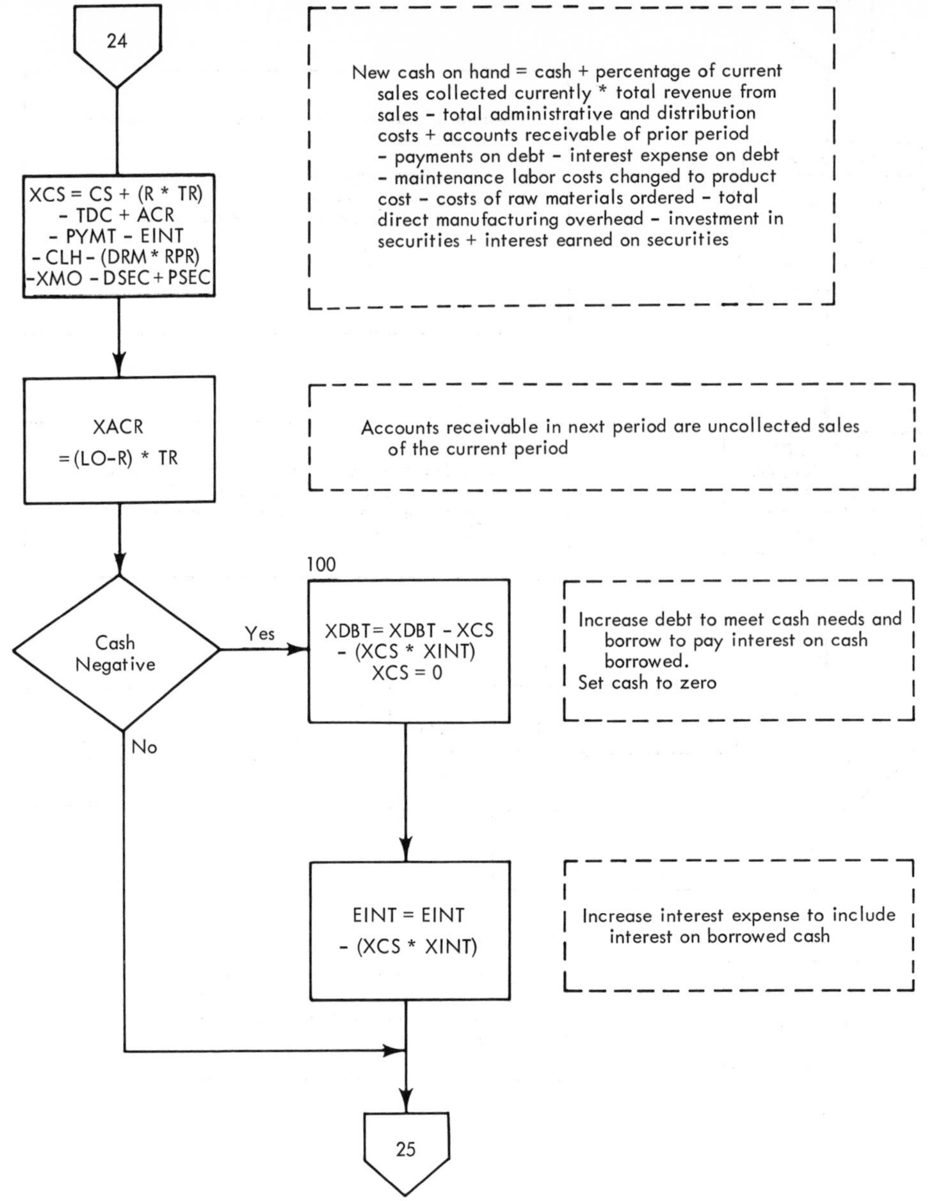
24
XCS = CS + (R * TR)
- TDC + ACR
- PYMT - EINT
- CLH - (DRM * RPR)
-XMO - DSEC + PSEC
New cash on hand = cash + percentage of current sales collected currently * total revenue from sales - total administrative and distribution costs + accounts receivable of prior period - payments on debt - interest expense on debt - maintenance labor costs changed to product cost - costs of raw materials ordered - total direct manufacturing overhead - investment in securities + interest earned on securities
XACR
= (LO-R) * TR
Accounts receivable in next period are uncollected sales of the current period
100
Cash Negative
Yes
No
XDBT = XDBT - XCS
- (XCS * XINT)
XCS = 0
Increase debt to meet cash needs and borrow to pay interest on cash borrowed.
Set cash to zero
EINT = EINT
- (XCS * XINT)
Increase interest expense to include interest on borrowed cash
25

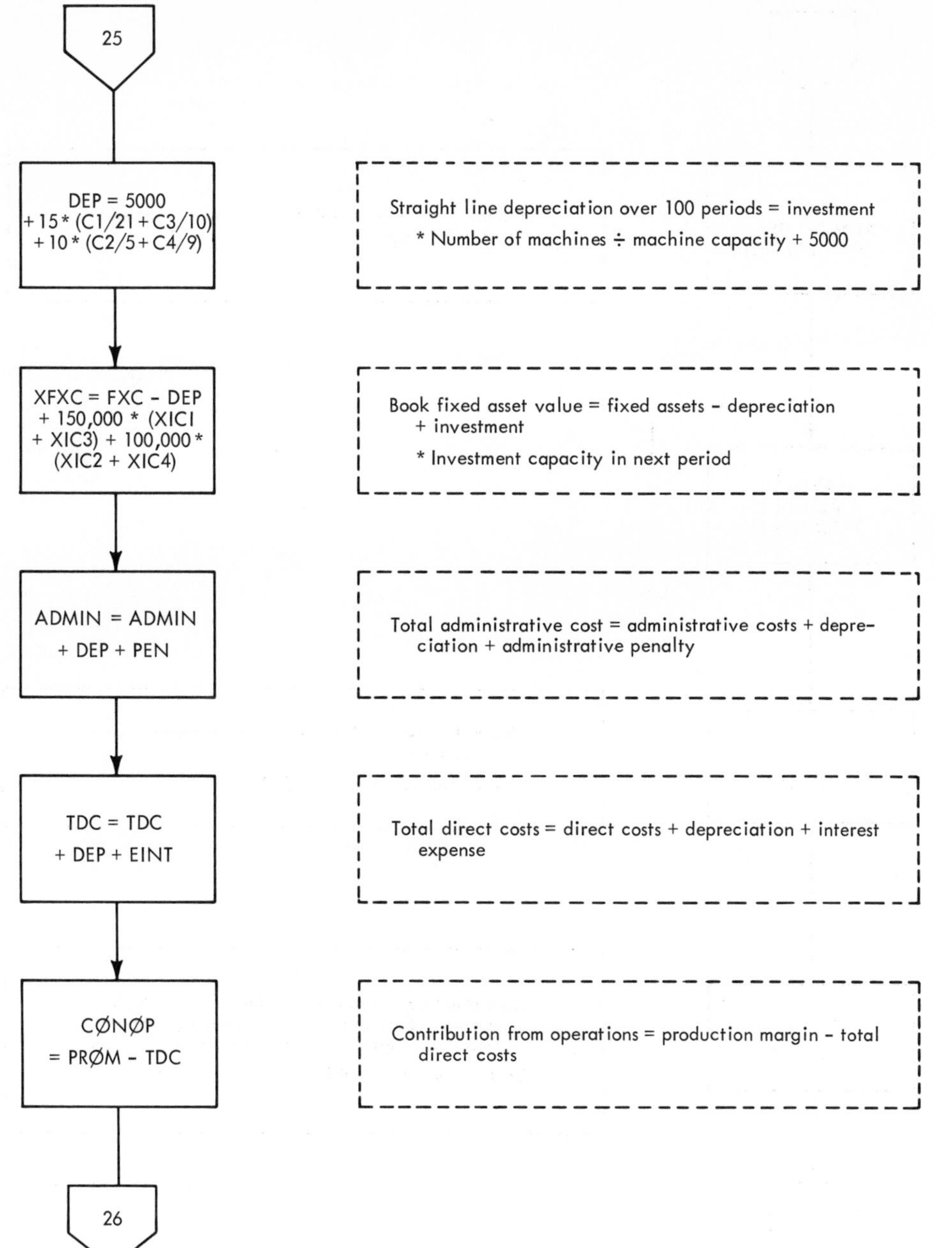
25
DEP = 5000
+ 15 * (C1/21 + C3/10)
+ 10 * (C2/5 + C4/9)
Straight line depreciation over 100 periods = investment
* Number of machines ÷ machine capacity + 5000
XFXC = FXC - DEP
+ 150,000 * (XIC1
+ XIC3) + 100,000 *
(XIC2 + XIC4)
Book fixed asset value = fixed assets - depreciation
+ investment
* Investment capacity in next period
ADMIN = ADMIN
+ DEP + PEN
Total administrative cost = administrative costs + depre-
ciation + administrative penalty
TDC = TDC
+ DEP + EINT
Total direct costs = direct costs + depreciation + interest
expense
CØNØP
= PRØM - TDC
Contribution from operations = production margin - total
direct costs
26

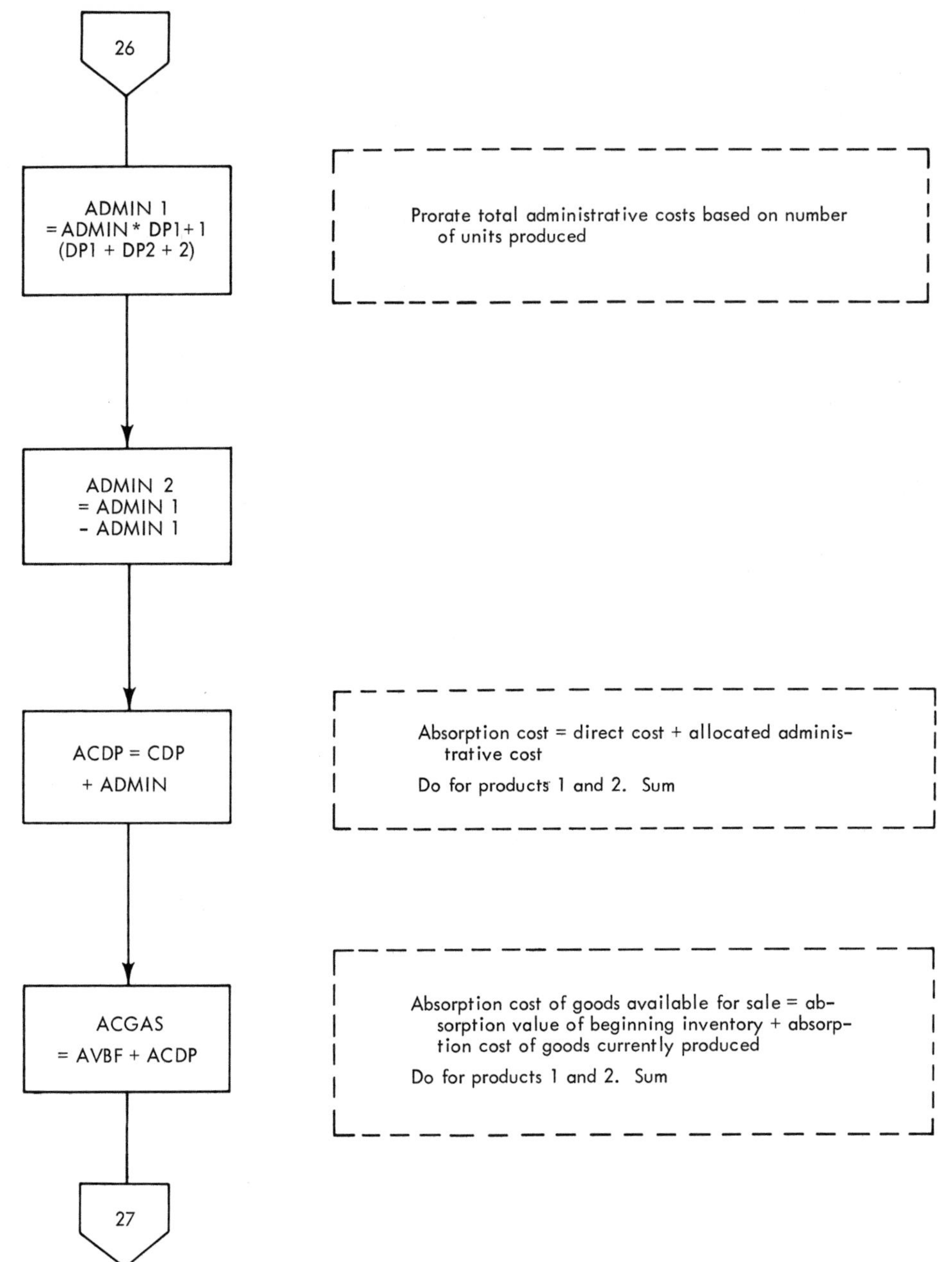
26
ADMIN 1
= ADMIN * DP1 + 1
(DP1 + DP2 + 2)
Prorate total administrative costs based on number of units produced
ADMIN 2
= ADMIN 1
- ADMIN 1
ACDP = CDP
+ ADMIN
Absorption cost = direct cost + allocated administrative cost
Do for products 1 and 2. Sum
ACGAS
= AVBF + ACDP
Absorption cost of goods available for sale = absorption value of beginning inventory + absorption cost of goods currently produced
Do for products 1 and 2. Sum
27

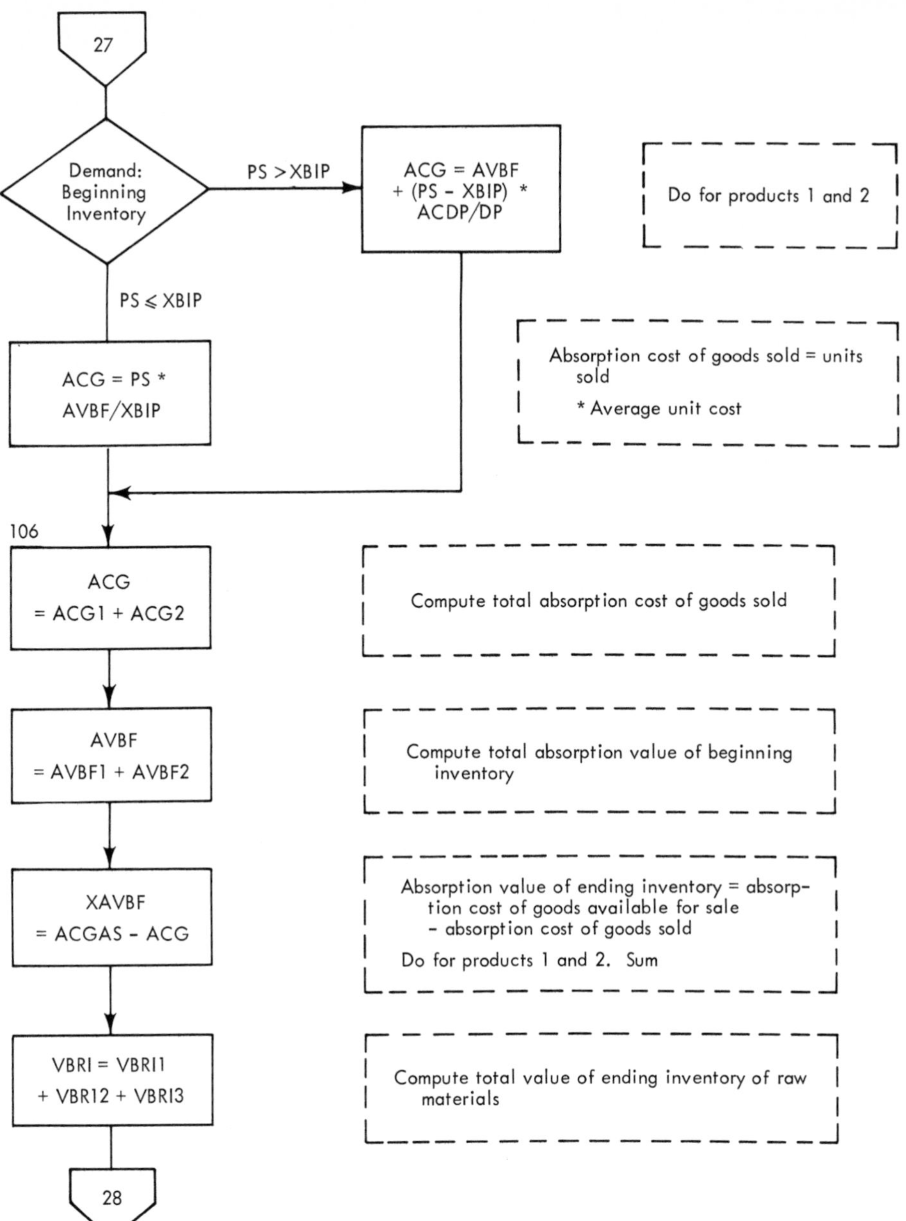
27
Demand:
Beginning
Inventory
PS > XBIP
ACG = AVBF
+ (PS - XBIP) *
ACDP/DP
Do for products 1 and 2
PS ≤ XBIP
ACG = PS *
AVBF/XBIP
Absorption cost of goods sold = units sold
* Average unit cost
106
ACG
= ACG1 + ACG2
Compute total absorption cost of goods sold
AVBF
= AVBF1 + AVBF2
Compute total absorption value of beginning inventory
XAVBF
= ACGAS - ACG
Absorption value of ending inventory = absorption cost of goods available for sale - absorption cost of goods sold
Do for products 1 and 2. Sum
VBRI = VBRI1
+ VBRI2 + VBRI3
Compute total value of ending inventory of raw materials
28

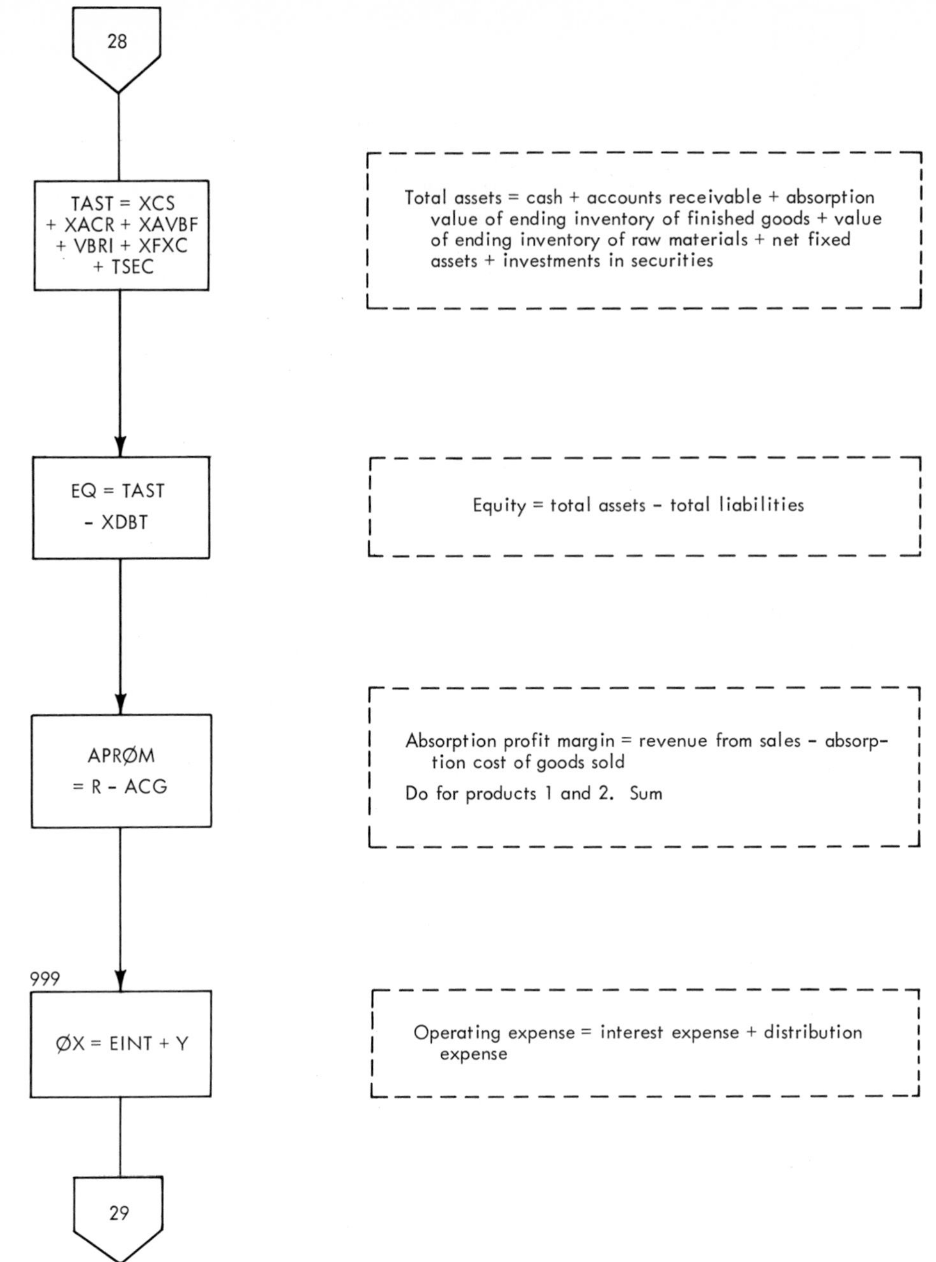
28
TAST = XCS + XACR + XAVBF + VBRI + XFXC + TSEC
Total assets = cash + accounts receivable + absorption value of ending inventory of finished goods + value of ending inventory of raw materials + net fixed assets + investments in securities
EQ = TAST - XDBT
Equity = total assets - total liabilities
APRØM = R - ACG
Absorption profit margin = revenue from sales - absorption cost of goods sold
Do for products 1 and 2. Sum
999
ØX = EINT + Y
Operating expense = interest expense + distribution expense
29

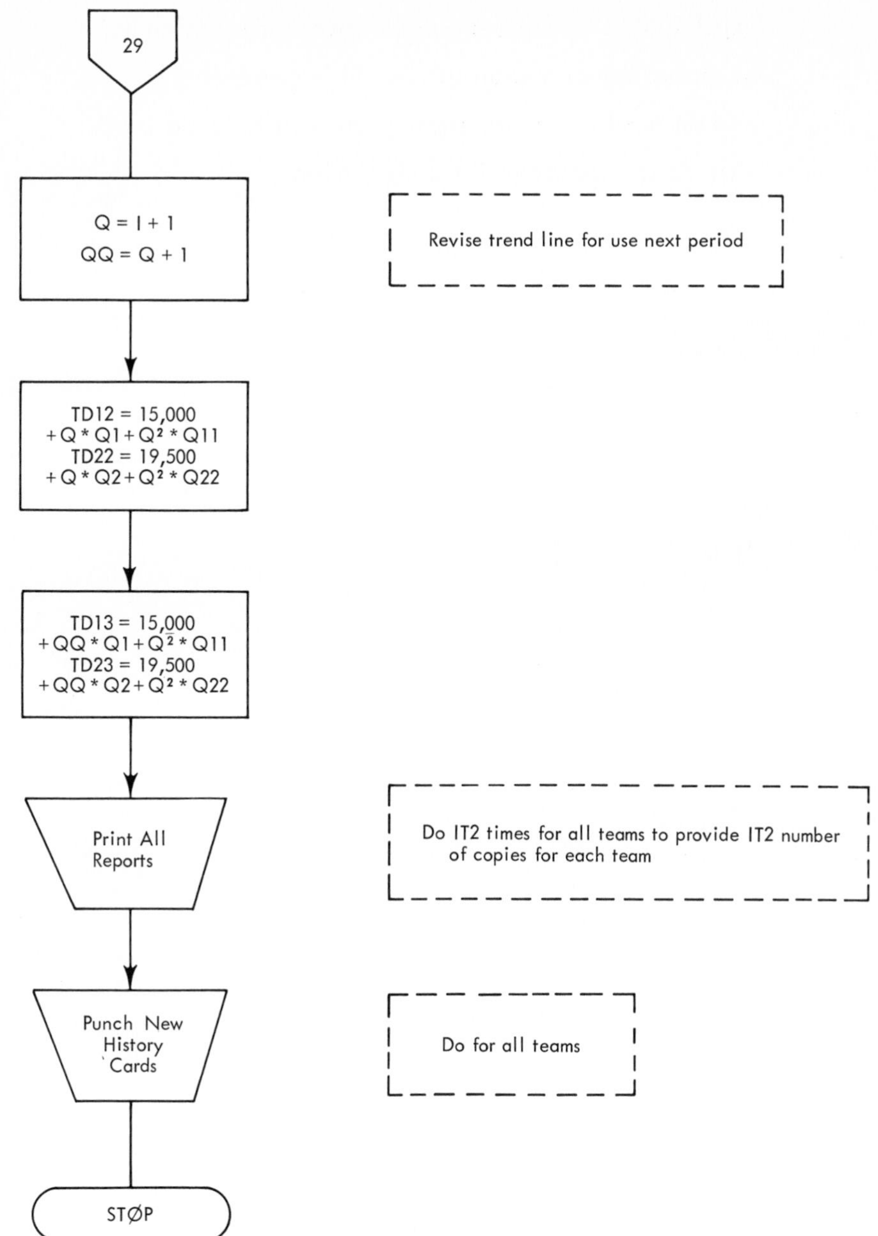
29
Q = I + 1
QQ = Q + 1
Revise trend line for use next period
TD12 = 15,000
+ Q * Q1 + Q² * Q11
TD22 = 19,500
+ Q * Q2 + Q² * Q22
TD13 = 15,000
+ QQ * Q1 + Q² * Q11
TD23 = 19,500
+ QQ * Q2 + Q² * Q22
Print All
Reports
Do IT2 times for all teams to provide IT2 number
of copies for each team
Punch New
History
Cards
Do for all teams
STØP

RANDØM is a random number generator which is incorporated as a subroutine. This generates a random number of two significant digits to be used with various probability distributions.

APPENDIX D

Information for Fortran Program Diagnostics

Introduction

The OPSIM program is written in basic Fortran. Routines are carefully adapted to the most basic of Fortran statements, so that most computer systems can successfully compile the program and process the input history and decisions. As a consequence with minor modifications, the OPSIM program should run on most IBM 700/7000 and 360 series computers. Most other well known systems can also successfully employ OPSIM, for example the Burroughs B 5500, the CDC 3600, 3800.

For computers with low storage capacity, program segmentation may be necessary. The following discussion centers around some of the pertinent features of OPSIM and the changes that may be necessary for a given computer system.

Input-Output Statements

Standard Fortran II input-output statements are utilized in the OPSIM program. Some compilers may translate only Fortran IV into machine language. In such cases, the changes indicated below should be made throughout the program.

Present Fortran II Input-Output Statement	Change to Fortran IV
READ Y,	READ (X, Y)*
PRINT Y,	WRITE (X, Y)
PUNCH Y,	PUNCH (X, Y)

*Where "X" refers to the appropriate input unit number and "Y" is the FORMAT number.

Control or Branching Statements

The OPSIM program uses the following control statements:

(1) the arithmetic "IF" statement; (2) the unconditional "GOTO" statement; and (3) the computed "GOTO" statement. Nearly all Fortran compilers will translate these statements into machine language for execution. The general forms of these statements are shown below:

Statement	Form*
1. The arithmetic "IF"	IF (a-b) Y_1, Y_2, Y_3
2. The unconditional "GOTO"	GOTOY
3. The computed "GOTO"	GOTO (Y_1, Y_2, ...Y_n)

The Random Number Generator

The source program is followed directly by a subroutine which generates random numbers. These random numbers are used throughout the program to create a "risk" environment for OPSIM.

Many software systems have built-in random number generators; however, to ensure the uniform performance of the OPSIM program, the random number generator subroutine is designed to be used on any compiler. A word of caution is advisable; some compilers require that the source program be separated from the random number subroutine by a control card. The computer center personnel can quickly place the correct control card in its proper position in front of the first card of the random number subroutine (between cards number 503 and 504). This control card now becomes part of the main deck and does not need to be disturbed for additional executions. Remember, this control card is in addition to the normal control cards already mention in Chapter IV.

IBM 1620 Systems

Many IBM 1620 computers have "disk" arrangements which allow use of the standard Fortran program with printed decision output. However, even where these modifications have been made, 1620 systems 40 K lack sufficient core and require program segmentation. A number of places exist for segmentation in the basic OPSIM program and it can be tailored to particular systems.

Where 1620 output is still punched cards, a modified program is necessary. The "modified" program makes use of "punch" output statements and has altered format statements so that no more than 80 spaces (or columns) are used per line. Two types of punched output are now given by the "modified" program: first, the regular history cards; and second, the decision output cards which must be converted to printouts via an accounting machine. <u>This modified source program can be acquired</u>, instead of the regular program, upon adoption of *The Decision Making Game*.

Special Game Modifications

Standard modifications are available for those users who wish special features in *The Decision Making Game*. For example, although it violates the basic philosophy of OPSIM, the authors have a version <u>which allows the student to make price decisions</u> for both products. The demand for a product, using this program, is a function of price--but demand is still affected by growth factors and irregularities. However, the experience of the authors--after extensive experimentation--has been that price decisions detract from the student's interest in applying Operations Research techniques to the operating problems of management.

The authors are always happy to correspond with OPSIM users in regard to special modifications and diagnostics. *The Decision Making Game* can be easily modified to teach specific lessons, and its potential as a pedagogical tool is almost limitless when used with imagination.

APPENDIX E

Cross Reference of Selected Subject Areas and Representative Accounting and Production Management Texts

TEXT*/SUBJECT AREA	SALES FORECASTING CHAPTER	INVENTORY PLANNING CHAPTER	PRODUCT MIX CAPACITY ALLOCATION CHAPTER
Elementary Managerial Cost			
1. Bierman and Drebin	8	8	-
2. Black, Champion & Brown	20	13	
3. Horngren	6, 17	17	17
4. Seiler	28	20, 28	
5. Vance and Taussig		10	
Production Management			
6. Bowman and Fetter	11	9	3
7. Buffa	16	15	Appendix B
8. Garrett and Silver	9	10	3
9. Hopeman	12	4, 14	12
10. McGarrah	6	7	8
Advanced Managerial Cost			
11. Horngren	5, 26	16	28
12. Knight and Weimwurm	4, 7	7	7
13. Moore and Jaedicke	16	11, 17	22
14. Shillinglaw	2	23	21

*The full citation for each numbered text above is given on page 158

INVESTMENT IN PLANT & EQUIPMENT CHAPTER	CASH-FUND FLOWS CHAPTER	BUDGETING CHAPTER	STANDARD COSTING CHAPTER	DIRECT COSTING CHAPTER	COST VARIANCE ANALYSIS CHAPTER	COST-VOLUME PROFIT ANALYSIS CHAPTER
9	3	3	5	6	5	7
24, 25	5	20	22	22	22	19
14	4	6	15	15	9, 10	7
26	15	20	24	26	24	18
24	26	23	21		21	22
10						
2			21		21	5
4			22		22	3
						4
2			1			2
14, 15	5	5	6, 8	10	6, 8	3
13	11	1, 3	6	17	17	17
19	8	17	13	14	13	15
20	2	2	10	7	11, 15	3

Elementary Managerial Cost:

1. Bierman, Harold, Jr., Allan R. Drebin. Managerial Accounting: An Introduction. (N. Y.: The Macmillan Company, 1968).

2. Black, Homer A., John E. Champion, R. Gene Brown. Accounting in Business Decisions: Theory, Method, and Use. 2nd ed., (Englewood Cliffs, N. J.: Prentice-Hall, Inc., 1967).

3. Horngren, Charles T. Accounting For Management Control: An Introduction. (Englewood Cliffs, N. J.: Prentice-Hall, Inc., 1965).

4. Seiler, Robert E. Principles of Accounting: A Managerial Approach. (Columbus, Ohio: Charles E. Merrill Books, Inc., 1967).

5. Vance, Lawrence L, Russell Taussig. Accounting Principles and Control. rev. ed., (N. Y.: Holt, Reinhart and Winston, 1966).

Production Management

6. Bowman, Edward E. and Robert B. Fetter. Analysis for Production and Operations Management. 3rd ed. (Homewood, Illinois: Richard D. Irwin, Inc., 1967).

7. Buffa, Elwood S. Modern Production Management. 2nd ed. (N. Y.: John Wiley and Sons, Inc., 1965).

8. Garrett, Leonard, Milton Silver. Production Management Analysis. (N. Y.: Harcourt, Brace & World, 1966).

9. Hopeman, Richard J. Production Concept, Analysis, Control. (Columbus, Ohio: Charles E. Merrill Books, Inc., 1965).

10. McGarrah, Robert. Production and Logistics Management. (N. Y.: John Wiley & Sones, Inc., 1963).

Advanced Managerial Cost:

11. Horngren, Charles T. Cost Accounting: A Managerial Emphasis. 2nd ed.(Englewood Cliffs, N. J.: Prentice-Hall, Inc., 1967).

12. Knight, W. D. and E. H. Weimwurn. Managerial Budgeting. (N. Y.: The Macmillan Company, 1964).

13. Moore, Carl L. and Robert K. Jaedicke. Managerial Accounting. 2nd ed.(Dallas, Texas: South-Western Publishing Co., 1967).

14. Shillinglaw, Gordon. *Cost Accounting: Analysis and Control.* rev. ed. (Homewood, Ill.: Richard D. Irwin, Inc., 1967).

APPENDIX F

Description of OPSIM II

Version II of the *The Decision Making Game* requires each team to prepare two decision cards for each period's play. The first card has the *same decisions* punched into the same columns as in OPSIM I. However, a second decision card is required in OPSIM-Model II, upon which is punched the price decisions for Product One and Product Two.

Price Decision. Figure F-1 shows the two decision cards required for each team in a given period. The price of Product One is punched in columns 1, 2, and 3, while the price of Product Two is punched in columns 4, 5, and 6. Thus, the only difference in using OPSIM II is that each team must now punch two decision cards: the first card contains the same decisions in the same column as in OPSIM I, while the second card contains the price decisions of the team. The initial decision deck for ten teams now has twenty cards--two decision cards per team.

Parameter Card. The administrator no longer controls the product prices for the industry; therefore, the "price fields" are eliminated from the parameter card of the *The Decision Making Game*--Version II. The discussions on other parametric changes in Chapter IV, however, are equally applicable with the exception of price changes.

History Deck. The history of OPSIM II is no different from OPSIM I, and the sequencing of card decks is also made in the same manner that is described in Chapter IV.

Source Deck. The OPSIM I source deck has been modified for OPSIM II play. Administrators can obtain the OPSIM II source deck on adoption--*or modifications can be made on the OPSIM I deck*. The additional cards needed for modification of the Model I source deck and/or instructions for modification are available from the publisher or the address given in Chapter IV.

1 1 15000 20000 500000 600000 400000 8200 3 0 0 0 0 0 0 0

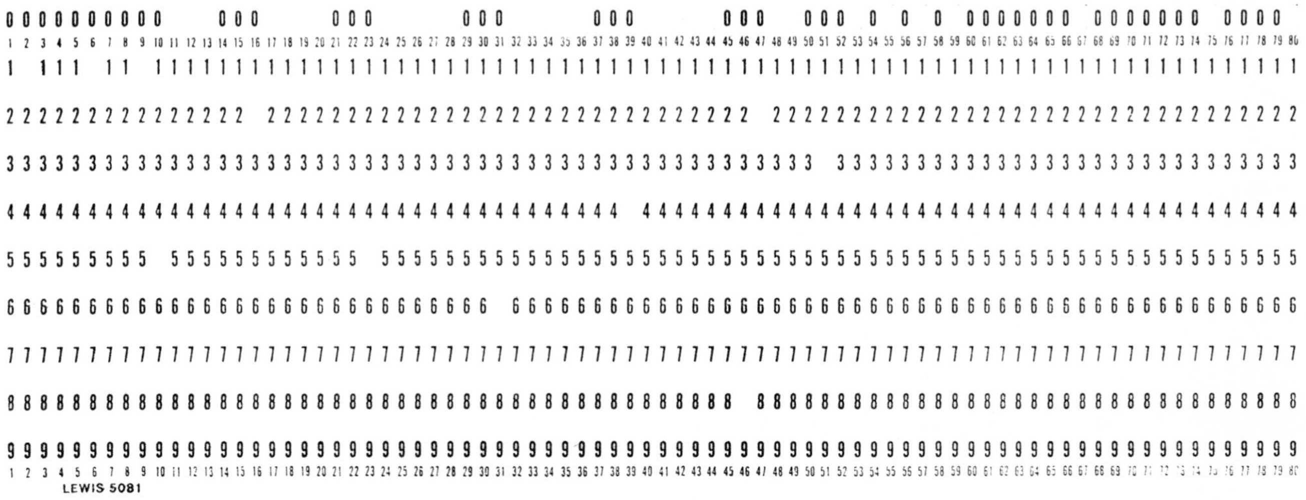

LEWIS 5081

1. Formats in decision card no. 1 are the same as in Figures 4-2 and 4-13, and the same decisions are made in the appropriate columns

75 65

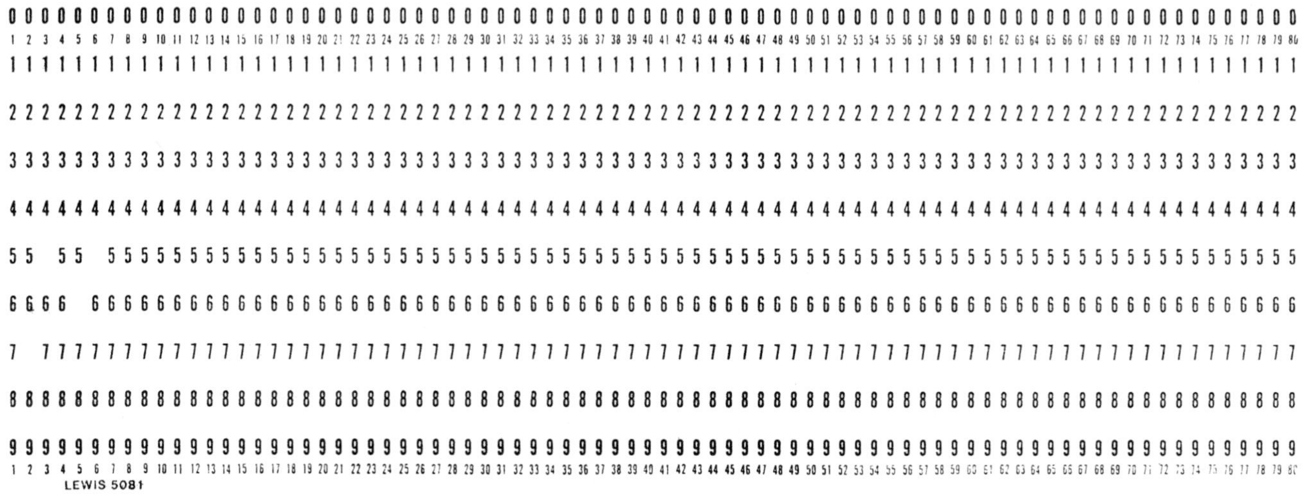

LEWIS 5081

2. Formats in decision card no. 2 are:

	Field	Variable Code	Variable Descriptions
cols.	1-3	PR1 (J)	Price, Product 1, team J
	4-6	PR2 (J)	Price, Product 2, team J

Figure F-1. The Format of the Two Decision Cards Per Team Required in OPSIM II.

OPSIM QUIZ - CHAPTER II

Answer True or False

_______ 1. If an investment in capacity 1 is made in period t, initial use of the additional capacity can be made in period t + 1.

_______ 2. To enter an investment decision on the decision card, the number of hours of the correct capacity must be punched in the appropriate columns.

_______ 3. Raw materials ordered in a given period cannot be used in that period; however, raw materials ordered do enter average inventory and carrying cost computations for the period.

_______ 4. Finished goods demand for a period can only be supplied out of beginning inventories for the period.

_______ 5. Only one machine breakdown is possible per team in a given time period.

_______ 6. Investment in machine capacity is from first cash, and then the residual is financed by debt.

_______ 7. Total profits and total contribution should be the same over the long run.

_______ 8. The OPSIM firm extends a 30-day credit line to customers and approximately 25 per cent of all sales result in accounts receivable.

_______ 9. Investment in short-term securities is possible with any cash surpluses.

_______10. In entering the maintenance decision, the number of workers is entered.

_______11. The number of maintenance workers used last period does not carry over to the next period and the number needed in the next period must be entered on next period's decision card.

COMPLETE THE FOLLOWING SENTENCES

1. Investment in capacity must take place ____________ period(s) prior to its use.

2. Total carrying cost of Product One varies directly with the size of ______________.

3. A unit of Product One requires__________ units of raw materials 1, __________ units of raw materials 2, and __________ units of raw materials 3.

4. OPSIM uses a ___________ ___________ cost flow system for inventory valuation purposes.

5. In The Decision Making Game, short-term securities are converted to cash by placing a ____________ __________ in front of the dollar amount to be liquidated and punching this figure into the same columns on the decision card where purchases of short-term securities are normally entered.

6. The OPSIM firm has production priorities which require that the computer use all available resources to first product the amount desired of Product___________. The remaining resources are then used to manufacture all, or much as possible, of Product ____________that the firm planned to produe.

7. All capacity investments by management of the OPSIM firm are financed by_______________.

8. Raw materials must be ordered______________periods before their use.

9. Labor hours scheduled and not used in production are stilled costed to the firm and are included in_____________costs.

10. ______________machine breakdown(s) are possible during a given period's production.

OPSIM QUIZ - CHAPTER III

_______ 1. The variable cost of Products One and Two include no overhead costs.

_______ 2. All of the accounts receivable shown on the period 1 balance sheet will be collected in cash the following period.

_______ 3. The production margin on the managerial operations statement is equal to the gross margin shown on the income statement.

_______ 4. The amount shown on the balance sheet for inventories of finished goods is the variable cost of production.

_______ 5. Setup cost for the respective products are included in the variable overhead cost of production.

_______ 6. The actual demand for Product One and Product Two for a given period is never known.

_______ 7. The setup cost shown on the Accounting and Marketing Information Report is for the next period rather than the past period.

_______ 8. The interest expense shown is the product of the interest rate times the debt balance shown on the balance sheet.

_______ 9. To the OPSIM manager the period contribution amount is more important than the variable production margin.

_______ 10. Period costs are not allocated to Product One and Product Two because to do so would distort the performance of both products.

11. The units of raw material 1 available for use next period can be found on the __________________ statement.

12. The relative standing of a particular team in comparison with the other teams can be found on the _________________.

13. The contribution margin for each product can be found on the ______________ statement.

14. The ending finished goods inventory found on the ___________ statement will equal the finished goods inventory found on the balance sheet.

15. The average cost of a raw material used can be determined by dividing the units used, found on the ___________ statement, into the cost of the raw material used, found on the ___________ statement.